Across the Red Line

Across the Red Line

Stories from the Surgical Life

Richard C. Karl

Temple University Press
PHILADELPHIA

Temple University Press, Philadelphia 19122
Copyright © 2002 by Richard C. Karl
All rights reserved
Published 2002
Printed in the United States of America

⊛ The papers used in this publication meets the requirements of the
American National Standard for Information Sciences—Permanence
of Paper for Printed Library Materials, ANSI Z39.48-1984

Library of Congress Cataloging-in-Publication Data

Karl, Richard D., 1945–
    Across the red line : stories from the surgical life / Richard C. Karl.
        p.   cm.
    ISBN 1-56639-912-2 (cloth : alk. paper)
        1. Karl, Richard C., 1945–   2. Surgeons—United States—Biography.
    3. Surgery—Anecdotes.   I. Title.

    RD27.35.K37 A3 2001
    617'.092—dc21
    [B]

                                                          2001027642

"An Act of Violent Grace" by Howard Troxler, on pages 48–50, originally
appeared in the *St. Petersburg Times*. Copyright St. Petersburg Times 1993.
Reprinted with permission.

To Eugene Corbett Patterson,
a man with a gift for writing,
a record of bravery,
and a talented zest for living

Contents

Acknowledgments   ix

Introduction: Across the Red Line   1

1   M & M   13

2   How It Comes About That a Successful
    Operation Ends in Disaster   24

3   Fate   33

4   A Columnist Comes to Work   40

5   Four Patients in Santa Fe   51

6   Hanging   57

7   Helping Sal—Knowing When to Quit   65

8   On the Table   75

9   Hotel Utah   89

10 Midwest Bulletin Board   97

11 Retirement Party   106

12 Match Day   117

13 The Norwich Classic Car Rally   127

14 Luck   138

Acknowledgments

The hardest part, they say, of publishing a book is to find someone, somewhere, who believes in it. I have been multiply blessed. Howell Raines, executive editor of the *New York Times*, knew me not from Adam's house cat, but sent the manuscript on to his agent, Timothy Seldes, of Russell and Volkening. Timothy took on the project and was kind enough to tell me that I had "an agent." When I asked him why he would take on such an obscure book, he said, "I'm old enough to do what I want." That led to the nurturing arms of Micah Kleit of Temple University Press and his sense of "let's do what's right." Russell Munson, the well-known aviation photographer, came along and threw his considerable enthusiasm behind the book and took the arresting jacket photographs. To each of them I owe an obvious debt of thanks; but more than that, I owe a large margin of respect and personal gratitude, for each of them is a star in his own league. They didn't have to do any of this.

My sense of principle and judgment come from my mother and father, Lucy and Richard Karl. My mother has always been a woman of purpose, and she instilled in each of her children a desire to work hard and make the world a better place. My own strong surgical father got me interested in his work, and I have tried to be as good at it as he is.

Eugene Patterson, Phil Gailey, and Robert Friedman, all of the *Saint Petersburg Times*, played significant roles in teaching me to write. Robert, with his droll approval, taught me to keep the tenses somewhat in the same ballpark. Phil, with his sense of connection to truly great newspaper/editorial page writing, has encouraged and suffered my sophomoric tries with grace and generosity. Gene, of course, is every discerning newspaper person's hero, and he is mine too. He is robust and generous and approving and has perfect pitch for life. He knows a phony at a hundred yards and he knows how to be brave without making a big deal about it. Just ask the Germans in World War II, the segregationists in Atlanta in the 1960s, or any craven public person who has found himself in the focus of his searchlight.

Nobody can write anything without a home, and mine is made by my wife, Cathy. She is the rare mixture of an endlessly supportive mate who has a critical mind and a record of successes all her own, but finds a way to honestly help me in everything. While some mates are dismissive and critical and others are patronizing and uncritically supportive, this woman is the rare perfect combination of support and protection. And she makes the best crab cakes, has her own cadence at the piano, and lights up every room she enters.

Across the Red Line

Introduction:
Across the Red Line

I am sitting in a patient examining room, on a stool with wheels, waiting while a 67-year-old man rummages through his wife's pocketbook, looking for his list of questions. I'm thinking of trying to write down what this is like.

His shirt is unbuttoned and he cannot see well without his glasses and his wife is trying to help but she is nervous and in the way.

"Take your time," I say.

I am in no rush. Already I see and feel some things that must be told. This man is returning for his first postoperative visit after having most of his pancreas removed. It is clear already that he is doing well—and few extra minutes for me to savor *his* health is just fine with me. I know the questions on his list by heart, but I know he must ask them in his order, so I wait.

I am working on a way to tell what this surgical life is like. I hope to fill you with the sense of it, the feel of it, even the smell and sound of it. I wish for a book of it. I've thought about ways to organize things, but every time I do, the form seems contrived and drains the color out of what I experience each day. Things rush past me. Extraordinary and ordinary things fly by in a jumbled way, so an orderly progression of chapters seems not just beside the point, but contrary to the point.

1

So, I'm going to try to tell you what a life of an academic surgeon is like in the new century. It is a lush and varied story, much different and yet still the same as known by my predecessors.

Like my waiting in this patient's story, I can tell you that most of what I do is wait and respond. The practice of surgery is different from writing or original research, for rather than constructing something out of nothing, surgery is responding, adapting to the problem presented. It is less originally creative, I guess, than composing music or designing a building but it is exciting, captivating and rewarding work and for me, thirty years later, it is still neither predictable nor dull, ever.

And I must make clear that these days, although I am dismayed that the costs of medicine are so high and chagrined that some surgeons seem to live a high-end lifestyle and appear to be out of touch with their patients and the world in general, I celebrate the rich privilege accorded the practicing surgeon. The surgical life is really about bearing witness to the human condition and about respecting the many almost whimsical variations of biology and about the intersection of the two. It is remarkable, really, the way I get to know people so intimately so quickly, and get to observe the brave and often noble behavior in them, while I witness the relentless push of biology, the aging and decay, the growth and development, but most especially the healing, both physical and emotional. It is this natural drive of our bodies to repair themselves from all injuries that is the centerpiece of medicine. Without it no surgeon could cut.

Another piece of this life is the satisfyingly sweet tug-of-war between the challenge and the reward, the difficulty of the case and its accomplishment, that touchdown, endzone, spike-the-ball feeling a brave patient gets when he prospers after a difficult operation. The residents, students and I feel it too. Or the remorse and agony I feel when it does not go well. This pain is for the patient, the family, and for me. It is intimate. Can it truly be that this sadness has its own interior fulfillment?

Then there is the university medical school life—one of lectures and papers and residents and students and academic trappings. It is the young that make it all worthwhile. But there's also the political infighting, the jealousies and the small-mindedness. You should know about them, too. Even though the philosophers and historians often find medical school to be not much more than a glorified trade school (I work with my hands, after all), I get all the expectant joy and tribulation attendant to raising the young—all the while aware that I am participating in the education of the woman or man who may one day operate on me. I hope we are both doing a good job.

Finally, can I possibly explain the camaraderie and elation, the black humor and shared care that makes this life of surgery and medicine so full? Each of my colleagues and every one of the surgical residents has sought out this way of living and they are, for the most part, straightforward, generally optimistic souls, who have seen and felt many of the things that so move me. I can say to one of them, "you know that place under the pancreas where the portal vein sits? You know how badly it can bleed there?" and I can tell from her eyes that she knows exactly what I mean and that no further explanation or description would add to her knowingness.

I would like you to know about that place and about the connection I feel with it and these craftsmen and our apprentices. To know about that place and those people is to know about things that most people don't think about. It just never comes into conscious thought.

Most of us go about our lives with this remarkable lack of awareness about the extraordinary "ordinary" health we enjoy and many don't want to pull that curtain back. But even today a few of us will start moving from health to illness. We'll see what we didn't choose to see—the business end of medicine. This is definitely not like on TV.

We will go to a doctor in his office or in an emergency room. Although most of us will prove to have no serious malady and be told to take this antibiotic or that ulcer medicine and to drink less, get more exercise, a few of the few of us will not find such happy outcome. Someone's story will raise a doctor's eyebrow and some tests will produce "worrisome" results and plans will be made.

Some of these patients will harbor serious illness and will require aggressive therapy and some may die of one or the other.

A few who venture out this morning will not come home. An accident or a bullet or a heart attack will send them careening into a hospital and into the maw of modern medicine.

About-to-be patients are reminiscent of zebras on the African plains. Lions stalk the herd, but it (and the soon-to-be patient) is unaware of the presence of menace. Then a twig snaps, a lump is felt or some bleeding is noticed, a car skids, and the victim is suddenly aware of a threat too close and so horrible.

And some of these patients, both those with subtle evolving symptoms and those with sudden catastrophic evidence of big trouble, will need a surgeon. For those patients the best chance of survival is an operation.

What that patient does not see and cannot know is that the surgeon sits at the bottom of this big funnel; of those who set out today, just a few will have a symptom or accident which brings them to see a doctor and only a few of those will need an operation. So, by the time they get to me, every patient has a fascinating and compelling story in progress. They are about to cross over a line—quite literally. In fact, outside of every operating room suite I have known there is a red line painted on the floor. Its purpose is to signal the point beyond which you may not go in street clothes; a scrub suit is required. The line separates the accessible part of the hospital from the "off limits" part. For those who do not work in the operating room, the line is inviolate. Only the patient and the staff cross over into the clear area that sits outside the actual operating room.

It is not the River Styx, exactly, but the boundary function is clear. The rational reason for the line is to decrease the bacterial count in the area surrounding the operating rooms by limiting traffic. There is a special relationship among the staff on the far side of the line. The intensity of the work makes for a certain forgiveness among us. Many who work in the operating room never venture out to the "civilian" side of the hospital. In fact, because they are going to change into scrub suits right away, the operating room staff comes to work in slacks, even shorts and T shirts, carrying their lunch pails. If it were not for the fact that they are mostly women, this group, chewing gum, could be mistaken for a carpentry crew. They, too, are craftsmen.

So the patient and the surgeon are the only two who cross the red line in both directions. And, on the far side, the patient is soon asleep. What I want to set down is about the crossing the line; about seeing the inside of another human being and, a day later, being shown pictures of his grandchildren. I want to tell you how the things I see on one side of the line affect the things I feel on the other. And it definitely goes both ways.

Coming down the funnel and into the operating room, any patient's final conscious act before a general anesthetic is the surprisingly cumbersome act of getting on the operating room table. Today's patient has found his list now, but I remember four weeks ago watching him lying on a movable stretcher, an intravenous running in each arm, trying to move over onto the complex $50,000 operating room table so as not to fall in between, struggling on his back to move over without ripping the IVs out or revealing his genitals. He literally had one foot on the dock and the other on the rowboat, but I have never decided which is which.

This is what it feels like to step up to that operating table and to take the responsibility; about putting out my hand, feeling the gentle slap of the instruments, laying my other hand softly on the patient so as to get my bearings, then drawing the knife across and through the skin, down, down into the person himself, doing the work, closing, then slowly walking down the corridor back over the red line to the waiting family.

This book is about the people who are the patients and the people who try to help them, about the beauty of the biology and the trouble that comes when the biology goes awry. There will be, I'll bet, a story or two about the resilience of human beings, and their frailties, and one or two about surgical success and surgical failure and about how that feels. Here please find the admitted contrivances and conceits this surgeon must employ so that he can bear to do the job.

My route to these stories was not unusual: I wanted to be a surgeon like my father since about eight. I went to college and medical school at Cornell, did surgical and laboratory training at Washington University in St. Louis, then joined the faculty at the University of Chicago where I developed an interest in cancer. In 1983, I came to Tampa, to the young University of South Florida's medical school, to help start up the Moffitt Cancer Center, and I've lived here ever since, serving first as founding Medical Director of the Cancer Center and now as Chairman of the Department of Surgery at the University. I am 56 years old. I love to fly airplanes, play squash, and bother my wife, children, and dog.

I got the writing bug from Eugene C. Patterson. He's the editor emeritus of the Saint Petersburg *Times*, the largest Florida newspaper. Gene Patterson worked his way across Germany as a tank commander for General George Patton, went into the newspaper business after the war and won the Pulitzer Prize while he was editor of the Atlanta *Constitution* during the sixties, when he broke with most white southern editors and became, along with Ralph McGill and others, a courageous champion for integration and racial equality. Strong and possessed of an enabling charm, Gene encouraged me to write from the moment I met him as a member of the Moffitt Cancer Center's Board of Directors.

I'd often tell Gene stories from the operating room or lecture hall and he'd say, "Write it down!" One night over dinner I asked him if I should take a writing class. "Hell no!" he said, "Just write and write and write and remember: English is a guttural language." I've tried to do just that. There are no long or arcane words in what follows.

I'll start these stories by letting you listen in to my introduction to third-year medical students as they start out their clinical life. These wonderful doctors-in-the-making have just finished the first two years of medical school, which consists of classroom learning, for the most part, of biochemistry, physiology, pathology and an introduction to medicine. They have come to medical school right out of college and they are about to be whiplashed into a new life. It is always in July and it is always hot and humid in Florida when I meet them in a classroom on a Monday morning.

Introduction to the Third-Year Class

Good morning.

You are about to experience the most rapid growth and learning of your life. You will be turning away from your friends and family and you will be joining another social order. No amount of careful explanation or patient description will allow those familiar with your original moorings to fully comprehend the life you are joining. They may respect you, envy you, be proud of you, but they cannot know what you will know. You are privileged.

Those of you here today drew the short straw: you are starting your clinical life on the Surgery Service. This has some obvious disadvantages. The Surgery Service is the most demanding in terms of time. You will probably get up at 4:00 A.M. and not get home until after 8:00 that night. Unless you're on call. In that case you'll get home the next *night around 8:00. Surgeons tend to be less measured in their medicine. They are big and forceful, sometimes curt and gruff. There will be very little time for reading. All through high school, college, and the first two years of medical school, you succeeded because you learned to read and study and practice and then pass the test. Now you will have no time for all the warm-up. Questions will dart out of an attending surgeon's mouth and there will be no place to hide, no way to think it over, write an essay about the topic. It is not a relaxing business, this starting on the surgery service.*

On the other hand, there are some advantages. You're jumping right into the fire. You'll know soon as to whether you've got the stamina. You'll become immediately comfortable with the thought of touching another human being in an effort to make them well. Internal medicine doctors are much more cerebral and often touch the patient only in a ceremonial way. You'll be touching them in a therapeutic way, and you'll be surprised as to how reassuring it is to both you and the patient that touching is required for the getting better.

There's a certain relaxation of the rules in surgery that invites intimacy. You'll get into the operating room. The social norms there will take your breath away. You'll be one of those in scrub suits standing so close to one another that you will touch each other without thinking about it. As for the patient, you'll touch another human being in a way that beggars description.

You will witness the basic optimism of surgeons. You can't do this kind of work without some form of basic belief that it is all going to turn out okay. And you will watch how different surgeons handle the defeat in times when it doesn't all turn out well.

Bid your family and friends farewell, for you will soon see what they do not. In the next eight weeks, one of you in this room will see a human being die on an operating table or in an emergency room. You will be changed forever by that experience. You will know that life is fragile in a way that your family pays homage to but doesn't really understand. You will see somebody your age, who left the house this morning expecting to be home by six, but finds himself looking up at you in fear from an articulated table under bright lights. As you look down at him with a fear of your own, you will slowly realize that he can't move either leg.

No on else in your high school class will know these sights. You are just 26. Your proud mother has no idea as to the earthly business of medicine. She does not know that you will start to wonder exactly what the urine looked like. She will not be reassured when you tell her that your physician forebears wanted to know what it tasted like. Patients will tell you secrets. You will watch a brave 45-year-old father prepare his wife and children for his death by a rare and undeserved cancer. How can he be so strong, you wonder.

I know you worry about the lifestyle of a surgeon. Your teachers seem like madmen, coming in early and leaving very late. They are fierce and determined. Their intensity scares you. I'll admit, it scares me, too. I know them well, but the size of their presence takes me aback sometimes.

Remember that they are like all the rest of us, scared and puzzled. I know they work too hard. I'd like for them to work less, have more perspective, more measure to their healing. But it is hard to stop. When you've worked long and hard to develop a reputation as a good surgeon, how do you turn down a referral of a good and challenging case? Isn't that what you've been bred and trained for?

The surgical residents are even more driven. They've dreamed of being surgeons for a long time and they know that they've got five to eight years to learn how. They work ungodly hours, bear abuse from attending surgeons, nurses, ungrateful patients and, if you're not careful, you. Yes, you can make life worse by not helping, by complaining about the hours they take for granted, by dragging your feet. Please try not to.

Also, try not to judge a surgical career on the lifestyle of the surgical resident, for you will never even consider surgery as a life. Look beyond the residency on to the life of the established surgeon. You may be surprised to see that the hours may be better than those of a busy internist. I rarely get to work before 7:00 A.M. and I am rarely in the hospital after 7:00 P.M. Just a short twelve hours!

I guess that tells you that a career in medicine is really a way of life. Doctors in the old days knew this in their bones. Their lives were forever being disrupted by the needs of patients. It has only been in the last few decades that physicians even thought to protect some time for being human, being a mother, a father, a husband or wife, a son or daughter. It is a natural tug-of-war. It is never satisfactorily resolved and there is no hope for an easy solution. When you leave the hospital and the patient, the disease and the healing go on without you. Every minute away dilutes the essential satisfactions of being a doctor, yet without some surcease you will soon be depleted.

Why not do emergency medicine? Steady hours, the drama of surgery, but a predictable life of frenzied healing alternating with time to one's self? It sounds attractive. I fear, though, for me, it would be little more than a series of one-night stands, a violent interaction of patient and doctor, without the introduction and sweet goodbye that punctuate the life of a surgeon. For me, it is just too detached, too impersonal.

So recognize that we're talking about a life here, not a job. Once you see it that way, it gets easier. Surgery is demanding, but it is doable.

You will see all sorts of defense mechanisms at work in surgeons. When you get to Psychiatry, I imagine you'll have some fun talking about us and our very obvious defense mechanisms. We need them, though. Nobody would dare pick up a sharp object and open another human being with intent to set right what nature or accident has made wrong without some sort of way to defend herself against the weight of the responsibility and the fear of defeat.

Some surgeons work too hard. Their defense is the premise that "If I just work hard enough at it, it will turn out all right." Other think too hard. "If I just read every article, if I just use my brain, if I just think as much as I can, it will be all right. After all, my fine brain got me this far, I must just think harder." Others have a well-developed sense of humor. Sometimes this humor is black in nature. Their jokes are best not repeated at nonmedical social events.

Others are relentlessly nice. "If I am just earnest and pleasant and friendly enough to my patients, the nurses, the clerks, it will be all right." These surgeons tend to court favor and admiration of all, sometimes at the expense of doing the right thing.

You tell me why you might like a career in surgery. The drama, the intensity. Then there's the critical nexus that the surgeon occupies. The surgeon is never trivial. You like the technical aspects, the machinery, the balance of the shining instruments. I know that these things rivet your imagination and focus your yearning.

You will need these glories to sustain you, not just during your training, but during your whole professional life. Surgery is too hard, too long, too persistent to endure without some sense of glory about the discipline. Allow yourself the sentimental and the celebrated drama; it will help you. It is dramatic and it is rich with sentiment.

Misused, these emotions become cheap sentimentality or, worse, excuse for sanctimonious behavior. Beware the surgeon who tells you she is holding the human heart in her hands. She did not build it; she's just visiting it, trying to fix it.

Surgery is not so much a triumph of the technical, but an exercise in stamina. Patients and their diseases and their families will vex and frustrate you. Your ultimate ability to help and to fix will largely swirl around your perseverance. Great surgeons have great capacity to hang in there. Somehow, they enlist their patients, too, in the job of hanging tight.

I tell our more athletic residents that the real pros get the job done under all sorts of circumstances. A good pitcher wins on a night even when his fastball is not working well. He doesn't win one-to-nothing, but he does win six-to-five and he may get a single in the sixth to help himself along. Surgeons need to win when the case isn't smooth, the anesthesia isn't seamless, the bleeding is more than expected. Once you've started the case, you cannot leave for lunch or call in a new management team. The responsibility is directly ascribable.

I know that the drama and technical aspects of surgery fascinate you. They did me, too. But that is not what captivates me now. I'd like to finish by telling you the view from thirty years ahead. The reasons I loved surgery are not the reasons I love it now.

It is the people, not the blood, the pathos. It is the people. The brave and singular souls who work alongside me. The braver and even more remarkable individuals we care for. There are hundreds of stories that can reveal bits of this life, but even in aggregate, they cannot convey the feeling of what it is like to pick up a knife and cut down through the fat to muscle, to enter in. In many ways the developing affection I have for the patient and my colleagues makes the job harder. It matters more to me now. Here are some stories as to what it is like. Take them with you as you begin your life as a physician. Take them as sustenance. Keep a few in reserve for the hard times. I did not make them up, I'm just passing them on.

I'll see you tomorrow morning at M & M.

1 M & M

"Did you split the sternum?" asks Dr. Stack, the attending trauma surgeon. He wants to know if the operative team opened the breastbone in order to gain access to the heart. "Yes," responds the fifth-year resident. He is the chief resident on the Trauma Service and this is his last year of training.

It's Monday, 7:30 A.M. We're at M & M. It means Morbidity and Mortality Conference. Once a week the entire surgery department gathers together in a lecture hall at the medical school. The purpose: to discuss each error, each complication, each bad result and every death that has occurred in the last week on all of the university teaching services. There are several teaching services. At the big municipal hospital the University oversees the cardiovascular, trauma, pediatrics, transplant service, and two elective surgical services. And there are several services at the VA Hospital and one at the cancer center.

Almost all the residents and "attending" surgical faculty are here—about 65 surgeons and surgeons-in-training in all.

Right now the trauma chief resident is in the pit, facing up at tiered auditorium seats that hold his inquisitors. His job is to describe the case, tell what went wrong, and respond to staccato bursts of questions coming from the faculty. He's learning to think on his feet, a skill that he will find useful at the operating table and at the bedside.

13

I glance at the Xeroxed sheets in my hand. The first two pages have short descriptions of the complications (morbidity) and deaths (mortality). Behind that there are ten pages listing every operation done by members of the department during the past week.

The case under review is described as:

> 24 y.o.w.m. unrestrained MVA hemoperitoneum, exploratory laparotomy, right hepatectomy, hypothermia, hypotension, coagulopathy, packs, expired in RR.

So that's the gist of it. From the sheet I learn that this 24-year-old white male was in an automobile accident (MVA —motor vehicle accident) and he was not wearing a seat belt (it is amazing how common that is). He had a distended abdomen when brought to the emergency room. It was immediately recognized that the abdomen was full of blood (hemoperitoneum). He was taken to the operating room, anesthetized and his abdomen was opened and explored (exploratory laparotomy).

I can imagine the scene; blood filling the abdomen, the surgeons scooping it out with their hands and mopping it up with twelve-inch by twelve-inch pieces of cloth called lap pads. There's a race going on. The surgeons must find the bleeding source and control it before the patient bleeds to death. But it is hard to see with all the blood in the way. Suckers are used to suck unclotted blood out of the abdomen, but some of the blood has clotted; this man's body is trying to stop the leak, too. Wherever the blood is coming from, it is leaking out too fast to be occluded by clot. So the blood spills out into the abdomen, covers the intestines, the liver, the pancreas and clots there, futilely, too late. The horse is out of the barn. The clotted blood clogs the suckers and must be scooped out by the surgeons who put it in a big sterile wash basin that the scrub nurse holds right next to the wound, for they are all in a hurry.

The sheet tells that the right lobe of the liver was removed (right hepatectomy) and that the patient got cold (hypothermia) first from lying at the accident site, then from the cool fluids administered to his veins in the ambulance, now from having his abdomen open. The open abdomen loses lots of heat by convection and this cooling must be reckoned with in all operations that open a body cavity. I know his blood pressure was perilously low (hypotension) and that these factors and others caused the normal blood clotting mechanism to collapse (coagulopathy) and he was not clotting at all by the time the surgeons got there. And now I read that they packed the abdomen with gauze packs to stop the bleeding by tamponade and took him to the recovery room (RR) to warm him under hot blankets and lights with the hope that restoring his temperature to normal would restore his clotting. It is there that he expired.

Despite the defeat, the chief resident is disciplined in his description of events, even though he's interrupted by faculty peppering him with questions.

It is a very bad feeling when the blood doesn't clot and the body isn't warm and blood diluted by saline infusions leaks from everywhere, even where no discernible blood vessel can be seen. It feels cold on the hands. Almost everyone in the room has seen this before. But there is no mercy in their attitude, no forgiveness in their questions.

"Did you put a shunt in?" The faculty man wants to know if a tube was put in the vena cava to control bleeding.

"No."

"Why the hell not?"

"The bleeding was from the liver, not the vena cava. A shunt wouldn't have helped." Score one for the chief resident.

"The literature shows that liver resection rarely works, it's better to pack," accuses a fellow chief resident. That's unusual; they usually leave each other alone and do not question one another. After all, each chief takes his turn in the pit and a hostile peer could do considerable damage. Maybe these two are feuding; one may have stolen a good case from another or maybe it's a private matter.

"The right lobe was macerated, it couldn't be packed. I felt we had to take it out."

No damage done.

"Did you do a Pringle maneuver?" asks another faculty member.

"Yes."

The Pringle maneuver is a way to occlude all blood flow into the liver from the portal vein and hepatic artery, two major sources of liver blood supply. But the liver is so vascular and the Pringle doesn't stop vena cava blood from entering it, so in this kind of injury it often doesn't help much. Almost everyone in the room knows this and they all must think it was a stupid question. The chief handled it well. He did not say "of course" or hint annoyance at such a trivial point. After all, the patient was bleeding to death right under his hands. Even though it is hard to remember what to do at first when someone is bleeding to death and you're in charge, this chief has had lots of experience by now. Naturally he would do anything he could to stop the bleeding.

There are more questions about the physiology of blood clotting, about how long it took to get to the operating room after he got to the emergency room, and about how long it took to get to the emergency room in the first place; questions about other bleeding sites, about whether the aorta was clamped in an attempt to raise the blood pressure, but to deny the lower half of the body arterial blood inflow. ("No.")

It becomes clear the chief did mostly the right things, and that this patient was probably unsalvageable.

So the questioners ease up and the inquiry becomes more respectful and compassionate:

"Did you consider the cell saver?" That's a device that sucks up the blood, washes the patient's own blood cells so they can be reinfused into a vein by the anesthesiologists in an attempt limit the amount of banked blood the patient gets. But it doesn't suck very fast.

"Did you consider" is much less hostile than "Why the hell not." The chief resident has survived this one.

This dead 24-year-old would be listed as an error in judgment: they wasted too much time taking the liver lobe out and should have packed earlier. It's not clear if the blood given to resuscitate the patient's circulatory volume was warmed properly. So E-J (error-judgment) is marked next to the case by the official record keeper, either the Department of Surgery chairman or a senior professor. There is no final report card; this is as far as it goes unless some unethical or malpractice-like event has occurred. It is harrowing. Even now as the attending surgeon (senior even!) I am tense when a case of mine comes up. Will somebody say: "That was stupid. You should have done this. Or that."?

Did I overlook anything? It is amazing how much fault you can find with your own work when you look back over a patient's management. Little things that seem so trivial at the time take on a huge impact when the result is bad. Should I have started a different antibiotic? Was the operation done too soon? Too late? At this stage of my career (the middle) my mistakes are rarely technical. They are errors of judgment. I am reminded of the old story of the young surgeon asking the senior surgeon, "Where did you get such good judgment? Your patients do so well."

"From experience," is the reply.

"How did you get experience?"

"From bad judgment."

Sometimes, if the resident is weak, the questioners get exasperated, intolerant, even harsh. The smart residents admit when they don't know the answer. Faking it is unpardonable.

Sometimes, the resident knows the course chosen is indefensible and he comes to the lectern looking like a dog who knows he has done wrong. Usually, the mistake is proclaimed loudly and the hair shirt is worn prominently. This is done to take the guns out of the hands of the audience—and it works, sometimes.

For the most part, though, each resident stands up straight, almost daring the audience to prove he or she did something wrong.

If the case has been badly mismanaged, the accusations pass up to the attending surgeon. After all, he or she was there and was responsible for the decisions, and has done the operation.

This gets very interesting, especially when senior faculty are involved. There is respect for the senior surgeon, but some satisfaction to the others that even an experienced and well regarded person can do illogical things or have a bad result. It is a much more level playing field than I have ever seen in the worlds of administration or business. There is a certain purity to this process even if the whole purpose is to examine dirty linen. That's the idea and the power of it.

The proceedings are not secret exactly, but only surgeons and surgeons-in-training make up the audience. The medical students used not to be invited for fear that they would misinterpret some frank discussion about a mistake. They may not yet know that surgeons are human. But now, I let them in. The process is so clean, so powerful, that the benefit to them and to us outweighs the risk. I have never heard of a university M & M discussion being used in a malpractice case, it is called "privileged communication," but I suppose it could happen. We are careful to throw out the M & M sheets in the wastebasket by the auditorium door as we leave.

Occasionally a great case of surgical derring-do comes to light by chance.

"What's this case 62310, the mesenteric ischemia?" asks the moderator.

The room rustles with turning pages while the group turns to the page of listed cases done on the emergency service. There has been no complication in this case, so it's not listed on the front pages. It's buried in the back between a gunshot wound to the thigh and a case of appendicitis.

"Oh, that was an interesting case," says the chief resident. This resident is just about finished with four years of medical school followed by five years of surgical training and he's one of the best. He's tall and poised and handsome and his dad's in practice in town and he's going to join his father in a few months. He almost didn't get a residency slot because his medical school record was only average and most surgical training programs are pretty competitive. But he got a job and has blossomed into a careful, thoughtful, aggressive surgeon. I'd let him operate on me, and that's saying a lot.

Now he's got the audience.

"Well, this was a 59-year-old gentleman who had developed vague abdominal pain the night before he came to the hospital. The next morning the pain was worse, and he came to the emergency room, and I just happened to be walking by and I saw he was in a lot of pain."

The residents sometimes walk through the emergency room and the medical floors looking for cases. They might find an "acute abdomen" (a perforated ulcer or ruptured colon diverticulum—cases that require emergency operation) or a patient with gallstones who might need her gallbladder out later on. Sometimes, if they have rapport with the nurses or medical residents, they can steal the case from the service to which the cases would ordinarily be assigned. This "trolling for cases" is held in high regard; it's thought to be a sign of aggressiveness and interest in surgery.

"His labs were all normal. I mean his wbc's (white blood cell counts—indicator of inflammation and almost always elevated in patients with surgical emergencies), his amylase (a chemical released from the pancreas when it's inflamed as in pancreatitis) and his liver function tests were all normal. He was writhing with pain, but when I examined him his belly was soft."

Wow, what a great case. Here's a patient with extreme pain, but no laboratory or physical findings to match. This is a notorious sign: this constellation of pain without the usual signs of inflammation is seen in acute deprivation of blood to the intestines—sort of a heart attack of the intestinal tract. If this condition is not recognized immediately and blood flow restored to the intestines, the bowel will die and so will the patient.

We know from reading the sheet that this resident knew that and moved to get an arteriogram (an x-ray of the blood vessels going to the intestine) to verify his clinical hunch.

"We got an arteriogram and it showed total occlusion of the SMA." He's describing just what was suspected: no blood flow through the superior mesenteric artery (SMA). "So we took him to the OR and took some clot out of the artery."

Simple as that! A throwaway line, "So, we took him to the OR and took some clot out."

Most of the room knows that you can't save a patient like this unless you are almost standing there when it happens; there is so little time between the catastrophe and when its effects become irreversible and fate is sealed.

So our hero says only: "We took him to the OR and took some clot out."

He might as well have said: "I was in the emergency room looking for something to do and I found this man in terrible pain and I recognized the situation for what it was and I got the right tests and I called the right attending surgeon and then we took him to the OR without a minute to spare and opened the artery and took out the offending clot and we were greeted with a great rush of blood and we then carefully sewed up the artery with plastic suture so fine you can't see it without the magnifying glasses we wear, and then he was sick as hell postoperatively but we stayed up with him, night and day for three or four days until he stabilized and then he got better and went home, normal, healthy."

He should have said: "I saw it, knew what it was, I did the right thing, I saved his life, you guys got any questions?" But he would *never* say that.

"Good save," says the chief. "Next case."

I don't know of any other group inside medicine (or out, for that matter) that has as its ethic a structured, organized, scheduled way to examine mistakes of its members that is so rigorous. And, in one form or another, this phenomenon is reproduced in each and every medical school surgery department in the country.

I take a great pleasure in these proceedings. I'm proud to be part of a group that has the strength to stare mistakes and bad results right in the eye. I think each of my colleagues, faculty and residents, recognizes that this is important, difficult work that distinguishes us from those who would rather duck the ascribable responsibility. I do know that it is good training for taking responsibility in the examining room and in the operating room. It's good practice for bellying up to the task. As a resident I was very frightened of these meetings. I'd read about the case, I'd learn the data in the literature. In time I learned that the way I presented the case could affect how I was treated by the attendings. Now, I still read about problems that I've encountered; and I'm a lot better at defending my decisions. I'm proud to be in the same company of the chief resident who saved the man with intestinal ischemia. I've never done that, but the others don't know this secret of mine. I have had lots of other grand experiences in medicine, but I have never had the thrill of saving just such a patient. My own life and experience has been augmented just by sitting with these people on a Monday morning.

I have thought that the president, his cabinet, and the leadership of General Motors and IBM, and American medicine itself might benefit from a little M & M.

But that's not likely to happen, and I'm not sure I know why. I do know there is a big difference between corporate, government decisions and surgery. Certainly the president makes decisions that affect or cost many lives. Yet when that happens he is pictured handing a folded flag to a symbolic bereaved wife or mother. He's got the marines, and the helicopter and the secret service to distance him from the decision. I do know this; he doesn't walk out of that recovery room after a 24-year-old motor vehicle accident victim has died; down the dimly lit corridor at five in the morning to the surgery waiting room to ask for the relatives. He doesn't take the family to the side of the room by the hall right then and tell them their son is dead. And while they cry he doesn't look down and notice, for the first time, the patient's blood splattered on the pant legs of his scrub suit.

After their tears, the surgeon dresses wearily and walks out through the big municipal hospital emergency room doors. They hiss their pneumatic salute as he leaves. No one plays "Hail to the Chief." The sun is coming up and he passes the fresh incoming staff for the 7 A.M.–3 P.M. shift, and feels the windless, warm, humid air. He's going home to shave and to shower and to get clean clothes and to come back to work, wondering, some of that time, if he should have done it differently and how it will go at M & M.

2 How It Comes About That a Successful Operation Ends in Disaster

Somehow, the phone is in my hand. My eyes fight to focus on the aquamarine numerals of the digital clock that sits on the chest by the bed. I work to make sense of the time. It's 2:24 and it's dark and I didn't hear the phone ring, although I know it must have, and I recognize the voice of the intern. He's excited, disjointed, worried, and, worst of all, frightened. My sudden awakening and the disorganization of his thoughts which are virtually pushed into my ear by his anxiety make the tale hard to understand, but I know something very bad has happened.

At first I don't even know which patient he's talking about. But he's calling about Joe Santo, a thickset 51-year-old, whose left kidney had developed a cancer, which had (unusually, astonishingly) grown right out his back, pushing through the lowermost ribs so that he actually had a skin-covered lump there. It was the size of a grapefruit. Usually a cancer in the kidney "presents" with blood in the urine. Not this one. This one announced itself as a bulge in the back.

24

Two days ago I had removed the tumor, the kidney and the ribs—the whole "mass" was about the size of a football. This left a big hole and the skin would not come together to close it, so, a plastic surgery colleague swung a muscle flap over to cover the crater. To do this, he took muscle and skin from the back of the patient, preserved its blood supply, burrowed a tunnel underneath the skin and moved the muscle over to the left and closed the hole. A skin graft was placed over the "donor" site from which the muscle flap was mobilized. Mr. Santo would be left with some loss of strength in his shoulder, but the disability shouldn't be too bad. This operation took almost six hours and we lost a fair amount of blood—not uncontrolled bleeding, but a steady ooze from the tumor's "feeding vessels" so that, in the end, we gave him four units of blood.

He seemed to do well after the operation. He was awake and alert. We were able to take the breathing tube out of his trachea the next morning. The wounds looked good and his remaining kidney functioned well. I was tired the next day but I had that good tired sensation. I felt fit when I saw him and spoke to his family again in the morning. I felt we had accomplished something. He had a pretty good chance, we all felt.

So what's the matter? "Slow down," I say to the intern. He reports that Mr. Santo's heart sped up suddenly, slowed down and then fibrillated in just a few seconds. A fibrillating heart's muscle cells contract at random without relation to each other and can pump no blood. The heart just quivers. The chaos can sometimes be controlled by drugs or shocking the heart with a defibrillator. The intern tells me these things have been done, that the fibrillation has stopped and that the heart is beating but not pumping blood very well: he is in deep shock. I repeat the same questions trying to focus on the problem. I wonder why this happened. Did we miss some telltale event earlier? Should we have done something differently?

"What was he like this evening. Before this, I mean"? I say, trying to sound coherent, in charge.

"He was fine. Good urine output. Good oxygenation of his blood. Normal blood chemistries were measured at 6 P.M. Stable blood pressure. He had some pain, but it was easily controlled with narcotics."

"How much morphine did he get?" I ask, wondering if too much might have depressed the activity of his heart.

"The usual dose."

The list of causes of sudden shock or death after an operation is short:

- internal bleeding
- a collapsed lung
- a heart attack
- a blood clot which has broken loose from the legs or pelvis and lodged in the lung circulation, obstructing outflow of the blood from the heart to the lungs. Since all the blood pumped by the heart must traverse the lungs before it can be pumped out to the rest of the body, the backup caused by a clot in the lung circulation (called pulmonary embolism) can be fatal.

It becomes clear I'll not learn anything more that will be helpful on the phone. I'd better get to that intensive care unit now.

Before I dress I wonder; should I shower now? Will I be back before morning? Should I take things with me for tomorrow? What are the causes of this sudden catastrophic turn in this man's case? Have I thought of all the possibilities? Where is the chief resident? Why wasn't he there?

Has cardiology already been called? Does his wife know? Is she dressing too? I have had this late-night frightened tired lonely feeling before, but Joe's wife hasn't. And this matters so much more to her.

I'd better get there. I skip the shower, don't shave. The dog follows me to the garage with that "What's up?" look of his. There is no traffic. It's almost 3 A.M. now. I am tired. The skin feels tight on my body. I want to get there in a hurry but I fear what I'll find. I am lonely. The responsibility for all this is all mine and it'll be a miracle if we can get him back.

The hospital is quiet. I park in the employee-of-the-month slot. It's open and I doubt the employee of the month, whoever it is, will be showing up before 7 A.M.

I take my office keys out of the car ashtray. I rarely use them; I stop in the office and fumble for my white coat. Maybe it will help. Maybe Joe's heart will be impressed enough by the ceremonial dress to behave, or maybe the coat will help with his wife if it can't persuade Joe to live. I walk quickly into the intensive care unit.

The resident and intern stand together rocked back on their heels, heads tilted back, looking at the electrocardiogram monitor hanging from the ceiling. The dark screen has green pulse waves and an EKG on it, some numbers and some lines, undulating, almost flat. The screen tells a terrible tale. The heart is beating but the blood pressure is almost imperceptible.

As I walk in the nurse starts, again, to pound on Joe's chest and the blood pressure tracing starts to make a better effort at depicting life. He's pushing on the heart and forcing blood around its circuit—the heart is flaccid. I can almost imagine it in its sac, the pericardium, not really pumping blood, just going through the motions each time the nurse squeezes it by pushing on the breastbone.

"Has his wife been called?" I ask.

"Not yet," two or three of them say in unison.

"Get her on the phone, would you?"

"Mrs. Santo, this is Dr. Karl."

"Oh my God, what's wrong?"

"His heart has stopped. We've got it beating again, but it is not working well. We . . ."

"Oh no. I'll be right there."

We give drugs to increase the blood pressure. But these drugs tend to excite the heart muscle and facilitate fibrillation. So we give drugs that tend to quiet the heart and prevent fibrillation, but they tend to lower the blood pressure. For an hour we oscillate back and forth—fibrillation with no blood pressure, normal heart rhythm but not enough blood pressure. Every few minutes, closed-chest massage is necessary to generate any response on the screen or to start a pulse in the groin or the neck. The resident and intern each have their hands thrust in these two private areas to assess whether the screen is telling the truth. They want to feel the pulse not just see it reflected on a green TV tube.

Just then Joe's wife bursts into the room. She bolts to his side, splitting into our group. She's hysterically screaming, leaning low, close to his unresponsive eyes and ears, shouting him back. She looks as if she wants to scoop him up and take him home to cure him herself. But she can't quite do it. She sees all the machinery and the strangers surrounding her husband and she steps back, eyeing the defibrillator and its high-voltage shock paddles covered with grease used to increase electrical conductivity. They've just been used on her husband's chest. It's the same chest she has, I imagine, rubbed, scratched, laid her head on and, for all I know, beaten with closed fists of frustration.

The nurses and the residents and I are surprised and caught off guard by this woman who has caught us doing these terrible things to her man. And we all take a little step back. There comes to pass a small pause in the effort. We look at each other, Mrs. Santo and I.

To her I say: "Mrs. Santo, let us work. I'll be out in a minute and let you know what I know. Please."

"Please take her out to the waiting room," I say to a nurse.

She is ushered out. I see her large son is standing at the doorway peering in but not venturing in.

Now comes the hardest part. In a small room with stuffed chairs that I have seen too many times already, sit three stunned, sobbing souls.

The daughter, about 30, overweight, anguished, pleads to me with her eyes. Her younger brother, a meaty, tall boy of 21 or 22, broods. He stares straight ahead, angry. He seems on the verge of standing and ripping my head off. I've met him before. He was quiet and concerned and big.

But just to my left in a chair sits Joe's wife, head in hand, sniffling. I sit on some sort of lamp table next to her.

"It's bad," I say. "We can't support his blood pressure. I think he has had a heart attack. We're doing everything we can. He was doing well. This just happened suddenly."

"He was having chest pain tonight—he told me," says his wife accusingly. I'm thrown. Nobody has told me this. Did they know? Am I out of it? Did this man trust me with his life and I can't even know that he had heart pain tonight?

"I did not hear that," I say, lamely.

"He had so much pain he gave himself lots of morphine," accuses the son.

Oh no, I think. He has had too much morphine! He has been hooked up to a "PCA" (patient-controlled anesthesia) pump, which allows patients to administer their own narcotics. It is carefully calibrated so that patients cannot overdose themselves, but it does require correct commands from a nurse. Was it done properly?

"I'll check right now. I'll be right back," I say, eager to get out of there.

The nurses deny he had pain. "He was sleeping, for Christ's sake," says his primary nurse. The PCA pump was correctly set up, he claims. I don't know whom to believe, but for now it really doesn't matter. I wish I was home, asleep, or at the dinner table with my family.

Two hours of effort later, Joe's pupils are "fixed and dilated." There is no life in his eyes.

"Okay," I say. "That's it, let's quit."

We stop.

An x-ray technician has been called in from home to take a chest x-ray to be sure a lung has not collapsed. It hadn't, but he was unsure as to whether we'd need him again. So he sits in the back of the room, watching, waiting, unobtrusive, uncomplaining. I wonder if he makes as much as $20,000 a year. He looks at me with pity.

I go back out to talk to the family one more time.

"It's over."

Sobs.

"I'm so sorry."

Stares.

"He seemed to be doing so well."

Silence.

Finally Joe's wife grabs my hand. "Oh, Doctor Karl you did everything you could. We felt so good about you. He wouldn't let anybody else touch him."

Joe's wife comforts me! This horrible failure and now this wonderful robust woman moves to support me. She knows, somehow, that I am spent.

I ask for an autopsy. I really want to know if I missed some other event; something not a heart attack, something treatable. It would be worse to learn that I had neglected something treatable. I need to know. I feel guilty. I have betrayed this man's trust somehow and now I ask his wife for permission to bother and disrupt him again, as if we medicine types can't get enough.

Yes, she says. He would have done whatever you wanted. I notice for the first time that her blouse is mis-buttoned.

"He blew into my life when I was 16," she says. "I have never been without him and I can't start now."

I walk back to the ICU. A sheet is just now drawn over Joe. The nurses are retrieving their equipment. The residents are at the nurses' desk writing down their version of the death. They record what drugs were given, how many times the heart was shocked. I thank them. We discuss some minor things we might have done differently. They are good boys.

As I walk out, the x-ray technician says, "Oh, Dr. Karl, I'm sorry." He touches my shoulder. This underpaid, hard-working foot soldier of medicine thinks to comfort me.

I drive home, sorry, sad, alone. Did he bleed internally and I didn't recognize it? Did he have pain and our staff ignored it, didn't hear him, denies it now? I'm glad I had him see a cardiologist preoperatively. I'd feel really terrible if he had had recognizable cardiac risk and I hadn't known or acted on it. I wonder, did we really take this seriously enough?

I am lonely and feel heavy and tired. I feel guilty and full of loss and dead broke and somehow, in some way, engaged in the thick of this life, all at the same time.

I pet the dog.

It's almost dawn. Maybe I can get an hour's rest.

The aquamarine numbers say it's 5:15 but I can't sleep.

For two days I worry about that autopsy. Finally, I get called with the results: He had a massive heart attack. The pathologist tells me he is sorry. "Thanks," I say. As I hang up the phone I wonder, just for a minute, how did I get here? How did I come to just this place, at just this moment?

3 Fate

There are times in medicine when I feel like a bystander watching a traffic accident. I have no direct influence over events; I cannot make widespread cancer disappear or restore function lost to a bullet's capricious path. But I try hard to force the foul ball fair with lots of body English and hope and careful attention to detail. Still, there are times when coincidence is so eerie and a patient's fortune is so inexplicable that there seem to be larger forces at work. This last year, the story of a man and his father has been unfolding with just this kind of frightening certainty.

Bill's father, Bill senior, died about 18 months ago. He had a cancer in the upper part of the stomach. He checked into a private hospital in town, got operated on and died. Bill senior was a prominent man in state government and then, later, he made lots of money in this town's biggest business. Everybody seemed to like him, and at the time I was vaguely aware of his difficulties because friends of mine would tell me about their friend, dying in another hospital across town. I heard that Bill senior had had the upper part of his stomach removed and then the remaining esophagus and stomach were sewn together. That hookup, or anastomosis, broke down and an abscess developed and required draining. Bill's father's weight faltered, then dwindled, and then his intestines became blocked by inflammation and pus. He died without ever eating again.

33

And so it was not surprising that when Bill junior had some difficulty swallowing during this ordeal he ascribed it to "nerves." But after his dad's funeral the symptoms persisted and Bill's wife and mother persuaded him to see a doctor. The family was now wary of the "carriage trade" hospital. They wouldn't say that anything had been done wrong, but they obviously wondered if Bill senior wouldn't have done better if he'd gone to the M. D. Anderson Hospital & Tumor Institute in Houston or Memorial Sloan Kettering in New York.

Bill junior seemed as popular as his dad. He'd been captain of the state university's football team, he was a talented lawyer and he knew everyone his father knew plus a generation of his own friends and acquaintances. If something was wrong with Bill, he wasn't going to be treated without some inquiries. That much was certain. Executives at Bill senior's company made it clear that Bill junior had access to the company jet, that no stone would be left unturned for him. If he needed anything, just let them know. But first a doctor had to be found to make the initial investigation. The family ultimately came to a well-known gastroenterologist at the university. He coaxed Bill into an endoscopic exam and that Thursday morning a stunned fatherly doctor looked through a fiberoptic tube and stared directly at a cancer in Bill junior's upper stomach. It was just like his father's.

This just couldn't be. Bill was only 42, an athlete. He was the son, not the patient. After some frenzied national consultation, Bill came to me. The family was anxious. The memory of Bill senior's illness, his operation, all the complications, the false hope, the prayers had not yet faded. Bill's wife and his mother had lots of questions. Bill, the still fit ex-football player, sat among the women, listening, reserved. They loved him and he knew it and he heard the answers to their questions. He kept their counsel, I could tell. I wanted the honor of being chosen as the surgeon of choice by a family that knew something about what they were getting into. But I had already learned about the extra worry and trials that attend caring for prominent people. If things do not work out, the failure is even more public than usual. So I didn't push him. But I was pleased when they chose me.

After lengthy preoperative discussions about risks and recovery, early one morning almost a year ago he was anesthetized. I opened his abdomen first. As expected I could just barely feel the cancer at the top of the stomach. Most of it extended up the esophagus into the chest. We carefully freed up the lower stomach so that it could be pulled up into the chest. After that I closed the abdomen, leaving the stomach and cancer unattached but still in place. Dressings were applied to the abdominal wound and taped in place. But this patient was not awakened. Instead he was rolled right-side up, his right chest was prepped and draped and, about 10:15 A.M., his second major operation of the day began.

I opened his chest, took out the sixth rib, found the esophagus and, at its bottom, the cancer. The cancer was dissected up and when I had about 5 inches of clearance below and 10 inches above, I removed the tumor, pulled the remaining stomach remnant up above the level of the heart and sewed it to the upper esophagus at about shoulder level. If this anastomosis held, his swallowing should be normal, but Bill would have to eat smaller meals more frequently as nearly half of his stomach was gone.

Young and tough and possessed of a quiet courage, Bill recovered well. He went home and started precautionary chemotherapy treatments.

None of his father's rotten postoperative luck seemed to plague the son, although every wheeze, hiccup and fever was carefully scrutinized by Bill and his family. They were on pins and needles. They had been here before.

After he went home, I saw Bill routinely for awhile and then sporadically in the halls when he came for his medical oncology appointments.

For months, after it had been decided to treat him with chemotherapy, Bill would come in one Thursday a month for treatment. Once his delightful, talkative wife stopped me in the hall to tell me he had just bought a white Mercedes. I knew he finally felt that he might make it, that the sword which had felled his father and pierced him might just be a little too short to bring him down. He was six months out from his operation. He might have had his father's cancer but not his fate.

And then suddenly last Friday, while out to dinner, I got paged and informed only that Bill had been admitted to the hospital by the medical oncologists. The surgical resident said his abdomen was distended but not tender. She thought the symptoms were due to the chemotherapy he had received Thursday morning. She saw no reason for me to come in to see him.

Saturday morning, without knowing why, I was drawn to make rounds before going to conference, even though I knew such a decision would make me late to our department's weekly "grand rounds." Maybe I was a little guilty about not coming in the night before. When I saw Bill, I felt better. He didn't look to be in a lot of pain. He was patient with me, answering with reserved grace the same questions the others had already put to him. He rarely looked me in the eye. His story pieced together. A week ago he had eaten too much at a political fundraiser (for a popular populist Democrat, so the food was black beans and rice, not quiche). Cramping abdominal pain followed, then a day of diarrhea. He felt better Wednesday, had a big meal in anticipation of Thursday's chemotherapy. After the "chemo," the pain came back and his abdomen distended. Something was wrong. I walked down to the x-ray department, expecting to find a set of abdominal films suggesting a stomach virus or some unexplained generalized intestinal malfunction common after chemotherapy. But the x-rays were ominous and they had been underestimated by the residents. They showed a complete small-bowel obstruction.

A complete small-bowel obstruction is a surgical emergency, for the intestine can die and if not removed, soon thereafter the patient dies, too. For this reason an honored surgical aphorism says that "the sun shall neither rise nor set on a small-bowel obstruction (without an operation)."

But now there were several dilemmas. What was the cause of the obstruction? Was it cancer? That was the most likely and most catastrophic cause. What was the risk of operating on a man two days after he had gotten a drug that prevents cells from dividing—a drug that almost eliminates healing and the ability to fight infection? Should I wait until the drug's effects have eased? Or was the bowel swelling, dying right then?

Then, too, there is the family. They've heard the words "bowel obstruction" before. The patient is quiet. His wife, terrified, struggles to hold on, be rational, be civil, be polite, be whatever it takes to make this come out all right.

I decided that to wait is to court the greater disaster. If he had trouble healing, he would probably survive; if the intestine died, he would not. I tried to be definitive, even though there were lots of unknowns; I knew that he and his family would drown in a pool of ambiguities and indecisions. So I said, "You need an operation. I don't know if the obstruction is caused by recurrent cancer or not. It is a possibility. A hunch tells me it is not the cause, but I don't know. I hope it's an adhesion. I think we should operate as soon as possible."

He agreed to an operation. I was all too aware then that I had two hopes. I hoped that I was right about the decision to operate and I hoped there was no cancer. These two wishes felt different because my direct responsibility was different. I could control the decision to operate and responsibility was mine. I mean, what if I had operated on him only to find the diagnosis was wrong and he died of complications? If he had a recurrence of his cancer, it is also tragic but at least it would not have been something I had done to him. I hate to admit it, but the first concern was more important to me.

The nurses and anesthesiologists were called in on this hot Saturday morning. The patient and family geared up—here we go again, they said with their eyes—but they were brave. Inwardly their hearts tumbled with that helpless top-of-the-roller-coaster fibrillation. All they could do was hold on to the cold metal bar in front of them.

I changed my weekend plans. As I walked down the corridor, I wondered if the timing was right. I wondered, if he had a recurrence, what that family discussion would be like. In the operating room all was orderly and prepared. Not one person questioned if the operation was necessary or properly timed. That was up to me. They were sleepy. There's a different pace to a weekend emergency case. We had no company in the adjacent operating rooms. Soon, he was asleep and the abdomen was washed. In a minute we'd know.

I opened the abdomen carefully, slowly, tenderly, as if by great care I could will this to come out all right. I was afraid to put a hand in and feel that hard gritty signature of recurrent cancer. I didn't feel any. An adhesion was found. The bowel had gotten stuck in a corner. Twenty minutes of surgical gentleness, and it was fixed. A firm area felt like a scar but could have been cancer so I called a pathologist in from home. He did a frozen section, examined the tissue under the microscope and declared it benign. The whole case took an hour. Now all we had to wait for was healing. We'd see.

But for this day the sword had fallen short.

As I walked down the hall to meet Bill's wife, I remembered suddenly: tomorrow was Father's Day.

4 A Columnist Comes to Work

I have some friends in the newspaper business. Through some of them I met another, a columnist. During dinner one night, he seemed intrigued by surgery and his questions made me think that he had some ability to discern and wasn't a reckless man. I told him he could come and watch someday. I didn't expect he'd take me up on the offer. I assumed he was just being polite. When he called, I was a bit chagrined. Nonprofessional visitors are rare and issues of safety and patient privacy are not well worked out. I promised to ask the public relations people at the hospital and the medical ethicist at the medical school. I would do those things, but I really didn't care what they said. I was just looking for time to think about the idea myself. I decided that if the patient agreed and the nurses agreed and it was legal, I'd do it. I'd had enough of the remoteness of medicine.

A date was set. The patient, a man with colon cancer that had spread, was scheduled to undergo removal of a focus of cancer from the right lobe of his liver. It does not seem to make intuitive sense to chase after a cancer once it has spread from the colon to the liver. His colon cancer "primary" had been removed almost two years ago, but a few cells must have broken off prior to or during the oper-

40

ation, and now a metastasis about the size of a lemon had been found on CAT scan. But there is good evidence today, accumulated from hundreds of patients, that if there are just one or two metastases and they can be removed with a good margin of normal liver tissue around them, then many of these patients will be alive five years later and be considered cured. The patient agreed to the visiting newspaperman. I agreed, too, as long as the hospital's name and my name and the patient's name were not published.

Driving to work that morning, I had serious second thoughts. The patient was a vigorous man, but he was in his seventies. Would the newspaperman consider all this expense for an elderly man a waste of money? The columnist could be only 35 at most. What if something happened? The liver is a very vascular organ and it can bleed like hell. What if things got out of control? Would I read all about a disaster in the morning paper? It doesn't happen often, but it could. (So far, I have never lost a patient on the table while doing a liver resection. But there have been times when a patient has been in profound shock due to massive blood loss that outran, for ten or twenty minutes, the anesthesiologist's ability to replace blood.) Would we make it look too easy? Although ten years ago I would be sleepless before a big case like this, I now do them all the time and most of the time the operation is a satisfying reassurance of technical ability. Does the businessman in seat 14C on a Boeing 767, reading his paper on takeoff, really understand the magic of lifting all that weight into the sky? Does he know the machine was designed by fallible human beings and is piloted by people who have, sometime in their flying careers, seen the takeoff roll aborted and the airplane stopped so short that the tires blew out? Will the workmanlike, undramatic feel of the operating room disappoint the scribe, a young man educated by TV renditions of medicine? I wished I hadn't gotten into this. But somebody needs to see what this is like. Otherwise we have a whole electorate out there voting on health care without much idea of what it really looks like when you can watch without the distraction of fearing for your own life.

The columnist was waiting by the front door. I took him up to the changing room, got him a pair of scrubs, helped him with his cap and mask and warned him to bring his watch and wallet, not to leave these temptations in the locker. I introduced him to the patient, signaled the anesthesiologist to go ahead and put him to sleep. I explained that the 7:30 start time was a coveted slot because it meant no waiting for another surgeon to finish. The newsman, used to the rhythms of producing a morning newspaper that gets printed late at night, looked skeptical. I noted on the patient's x-rays that he was 77 years old, about four years older than I had remembered, and I hoped this fact would not be discovered.

Our visitor followed us out to the scrub sink. Through the window I could see Sharon washing the patient's abdomen and chest. The incision is made in the abdomen but sometimes it has to be extended into the chest to get control of bleeding, so both are washed: "prepped." We backed into the room, slugging the O.R. door open with our backsides. I took a towel from Judy who was already gowned and gloved. I wiped my hands and forearms, tossed the towel to Sharon who had by then finished her scrubbing and was helping me and the medical student and the resident get into our gowns and our gloves. The student and resident liked having the reporter there. I could see ideas of fame dancing beneath their scrub caps.

We laid on the drapes and Judy wheeled up her Mayo stand and we took our positions: me and the medical student on the patient's left and Judy and the chief resident on his right. The patient was then in that anticipatory state: "prepped and draped." I told the columnist to turn away if he felt queasy and to remember that the hard part was the beginning. Once we're in there, doing the work, it is so riveting that it is hard to get sick. I made an incision under the ribs—a "bilateral subcostal"—it looked like a big frown on the upper abdomen. There was no significant bleeding. Next I divided the rectus muscle with the cautery (we call it by its trade name, the "Bovie").

Judy was ready with two Kocher clamps named after the famous German surgeon of the late 1800s; they have teeth at the end of them to grasp the just-divided muscle so that I could hold up the abdominal wall and see the adhesions of tissue which had resulted from the patient's colon cancer operation. The tissue in there was filmy, soft. Adhesions are just areas where tissue has stuck together in an unnatural, nonembryologic way. They are caused by the inflammatory reaction of tissues that have been handled surgically. Most of the time they are a nuisance only, but you know they can cause obstruction of the intestine.

Next into my hands popped a pair of scissors, Metzenbaum's, for taking down these adhesions. So far, not a word had been spoken. But Judy knew, just from the positioning of my outstretched hand, what I needed. She knew the drill. She delivers the instruments with a gentle flick of her wrist so that they pop into my palm. Some scrub nurses smack the tools so sharply that they make my hand burn. Others wave the instrument around timidly, waiting for my hand to catch up with it, even though I'm looking into the

wound. Our newsman backed away at first, but then cir-
cled back to a position Sharon, the circulating nurse, had
advised, near the anesthesiologist, just across the "ether
screen," that part of the drapes near the head where
they're lifted up high and affixed to poles. This arrangement served to divide the anesthesia part from the surgical
part. Ours was sterile, the other was just clean.

I asked Judy about her new boyfriend. A new disc was
selected by Sharon; the music is left up to her. Music in the
operating room? That's the part they get right on TV and in
the movies. But it is not as if the music is the score to the
operation. It is background only. It soothes us and helps set
our rhythms for the case. A smooth professional operation
has its own very real rhythm and the music helps us sustain it. Soft and quiet music played during the hard parts of
the procedure gives way to more up-tempo stuff as we
close the patient.

Now we were in and I could just begin to get the liver
mobilized. I cut the ligaments that held the liver in place
and slowly the organ began to yield. Finally I could see the
cancer easily, just where it was supposed to be, thank God.
The inside of this old man did not look that much different
than the inside of a 30-year-old—it rarely does. The chief
resident was joking now. This was going to be easy; I could
feel him thinking. His bravado made me anxious. I could
see it in the paper. "Just before this poor elderly gentleman
bled to death, the operative team spoke of their love lives
and joked without thought or contemplation."

I asked Sharon to turn off the music. I rarely do this, but
I wanted to impress the resident that he was getting over
the line and I wanted the newsman to see that this was the
hard part. Judy understood. We had hundreds of hours

together, standing right on top of each other. She knew what I was doing.

I took the Bovie and burned a line in the liver around the tumor with margin to spare. I took up the CUSA, a wand with a high-speed vibrating device on its end, and tested it by activating it with a foot pedal. The high-frequency vibration macerates the liver tissue but does not cut the stouter arteries and veins and bile ducts that are hidden in the liver substance. Using the CUSA I could "paint" my way through the liver substance and draw out the vessels before I cut into them and they bled. The arrangement of the blood vessels lurking in the liver's brown-red meatiness is remarkable. The hepatic artery and the portal vein enter the liver and immediately divide like branches of a tree. In the same space of liver, branches of the hepatic veins *collect* blood from the liver and come together as rivulets, then streams and then rivers, finally joining into three main veins which empty into the vena cava and then right into the heart. So the distribution of blood vessels in the liver is like several tree branches lying with their main branches in opposite directions and their arborized fuzzy ends hopelessly entwined in the complicated commerce of blood conduits. I asked that the Bovie setting be increased to maximum searing capacity. I asked the anesthesiologist if he was ready to give blood. I try not to give blood at all because blood transfusions decrease the power of the patient's own immune system and may make recurrence of the cancer more likely. But if there is a choice between a small immune depression and bleeding to death, we give blood and don't fret about it. I looked at Judy and winked above my mask. She rolled her eyes. In the next twenty minutes I would ask for instruments with staccato commands. She knew that I knew she is maybe one of the best in the country. She has in her bones what this is all about and she likes these big, difficult cases and I depend on her and we both love the arrangement. Okay, I said, let's go.

And we started in. I wasn't scared exactly, but I was wired; I always am. My sense of hearing is augmented. Sight, too. I can hear the door open or someone whisper. I have gotten more comfortable with this moment. Actually, I like it. But it is a feeling that borders on fear on one side and respect on the other. Respect for the job at hand, the beauty of the anatomy, the danger of the disease and the risk of the operation, and the privilege of being right there at that moment, in that man's life, in my life, too. The bleeding was brisk at first, but we controlled some of the deluge by squeezing the liver in our hands, compressing those thin-walled veins and preventing them from spilling dark purple blood in our way. The big vessels could be seen before transection, so we stopped and tied them with silk ties before they bled. Soon the tumor and surrounding tissue was out and sent to pathology for sectioning to be sure the margin was adequate. I knew it would be.

Now, with the remaining liver bleeding controlled, we irrigated the wound and closed the muscle in layers using stout plastic suture. I did not know if the whole thing looked complicated or simple. I did not know if our newsman was impressed or bored. I could not tell if he felt we were arrogant carpenters who had no great skill other than self-importance, or if he could see the danger and the fear in me. Would he sneer or applaud? If he applauded would it be for the right reason? Had he really seen?

He called the next day and left a message. I called back about 4 P.M. and he was there.

"Hi," I said.

"Hey," he said, "I had a great time yesterday. I'd just like to ask you a few questions."

"Okay."

"The patient was pretty old, wasn't he? I think I called him 'elderly' in the column I'm writing."

Oh, shit, I thought. He's going to say we wasted money on this poor old guy. The patient was doing fine and I knew he'd be all right physically, but was he going to have to read that he wasn't worth the cash in the paper? Was I going to be made out to be a money-hungry, operate-on-anybody-for-hire kind of guy? (I get a university salary, by the way, which is negotiated each year and is not a direct percentage of monies collected by the university in my name.)

"How about 'retired,'" I offered.

"Okay," he said

"You told the family you got it all, but could it come back?'

Oh, man, this was going to be a disaster. I never tell anybody "I got it all." Recurrences are too common. We can't be that arrogant. How did this man hear me say that? He must watch too much television.

"No, I said we took out what we expected, and that we could detect no other focus of cancer with the ultrasound machine."

"Oh."

Silence while he reread his column. Then, "I want to use that joke you told me about cures."

Again I was thrown back, speechless. I had tried to explain that what really matters in cancer biology is whether the disease harms the patient. I don't care if there are some cancer cells in a patient as long as they don't grow and harm him. Some cancers, thyroid and prostate come to mind, can exist for years in people and they live to a ripe old age and die of something else, a "competing risk factor" such as heart disease. To illustrate this concept I had told our visitor that we often say that we're satisfied even if a cancer returns as long as the patient lives to be 95 and dies after being "shot in the ass by a jealous lover." Great, now I was to look obscene as well as greedy and stupid.

I asked him to leave out the joke, or at least the obscenity.

Next morning, on the driveway, I found his piece on the front page of the second section of a newspaper that reaches about 350,000 homes.

An Act of Violent Grace

Howard Troxler, Columnist

So I meet this surgeon. He describes it with so much awe and joy that when he says come watch, I say, sure.

The room is maybe 20 feet by 30 feet, cold, green, filled with machines. It is just past 7:30 A.M., a coveted time slot: first at bat, no waiting.

The patient, a retired man, is asleep, tubes in his nose and mouth. He is painted with disinfectant and draped in blue sheets. His eyes are taped.

Neil Young's Unplugged *plays softly on a portable stereo. The surgeon stands opposite the assisting surgeon. They are flanked by the scrub nurse, with her trays of instruments, and a third-year medical student. At the patient's head stands the anesthesiologist; at his feet, a "circulating" nurse—she circulates, doing what needs to be done.*

The incision is a swift, confident glide of the knife below the ribs. What little blood appears is sponged away. We sure have a lot of layers, and the surgeon uses a pen-like tool—like a soldering iron, I think—that burns through the inner ones precisely.

The wound is pulled open and held by retractors. The surgeon says, "Can't beat this job. Indoor work, air conditioning . . ." The small talk masks much.

Now the organs are exposed. The liver's glistening, pinkish-brown surface is prominent. The surgeons free it from some of its moorings, then reach deep inside to pull it into the open.

They bring into view a small, discolored circle, surrounded by a gritty, whitish ring. "There it is," the surgeon says, and I realize: I am looking at cancer.

Waiting for an ultrasound team, the surgeons give the student a tour: the major veins, the diaphragm, its motion now beautifully visible as the patient breathes. The machine arrives, the liver is scanned and only the one spot is found. Good.

The surgeon admires airline pilots. He speaks of the "sterile cockpit," during takeoffs and landings when the risk is highest and small talk is forbidden. It is time for the sterile cockpit, he says. The music is turned off. He takes his tools and burns an outline a couple of inches around the tumor, as a carpenter might pencil in the line to cut.

A generation ago, one of five patients died from this surgery, the blood-rich liver too difficult to maneuver. Now death on the table is much more rare. A $90,000 machine helps the surgeons make their way through the tissue, isolating and clamping the blood vessels and bile ducts as they go.

Sponges are used, removed and carefully stored, to keep track of their number and of blood loss. The scrub nurse lays each tool in the surgeon's hand almost before he asks for it.

The cancerous piece is separated and tossed, unceremoniously, into a plastic dishpan, then slid into a plastic tub to be taken to the lab, to make sure they took out enough. They did.

The liver now has a gaping wedge-shaped wound, but is seeping only a little blood. The surgeon holds sponges against it until it stops, then puts it back in place, unbandaged, unstitched. The music is turned back on. The surgeons take pitchers of saline solution and literally dump it into the body cavity, like they were rinsing the dishes, and the student suctions it away.

"How are your knots?" the surgeon asks the student. "I practiced over the weekend," he answers nervously. He gets to do a few. There are two sets of sutures, pulling together the inside and outside layers of the abdomen's walls. The wound is narrowing, looking more and more like only a really bad cut. The outer skin is stapled together, finally, in a neat row—the doctors, now relaxed enough to joke, tell the student that patients will judge his surgical skill by the neatness of the scar.

"Thank you," the surgeon says, and leaves the room around 10:30. As I follow him, awe-struck, he turns and says, "Pretty crude, huh?" He finds the family waiting nervously in a small room, and tells them: Only one spot, and they got all of it. Tears of relief. Soon the patient is waking in the recovery room. He'll go home in a week or less. The bill may be $25,000, ballpark.

I know some will ask why so much is given to a man in his 70s on his second cancer. But this act of violent grace gives him time, maybe several years. Cancer surgeons say of their patients, "I want him to live until he's 95—and to die from getting shot by a jealous lover." That sounds pretty good to me.

—from the *St. Petersburg Times*

He got it. Most of it, anyway.

5 Four Patients in Santa Fe

Rob reaches down into a hospital crib and scoops up a four-year-old sleeping child. It is 8:30 in the morning, but the boy is still asleep. Next to the bed his mother rocks gently in the plain wooden hospital rocking chair; she blinks at the winter sunlight just now cresting the Sangre de Cristo mountains and sliding down the snow-covered mountainside into their hospital room.

"Come on, Josh, wake up." Rob is firm but pleasant. He doesn't placate or small-talk. You can tell he means it: Get up.

Josh has had hydrocephalus (water on the brain) and he has spastic legs. Two years ago a shunt was put in the ventricles of his brain and connected by a plastic tube under his skin to his abdominal cavity so the excess fluid in his head (a closed space) could drain into his belly (a distensible space where the fluid will be reabsorbed). But the shunt has stopped working and the question is: Will fluid re-accumulate in his brain, cause increased pressure and lead to new neurological symptoms and, if untreated, cause death? Or will the fluid not build up and nothing bad happen? How is it that the possibilities can be so disparate? Death versus no change. And the doctor cannot predict the difference.

51

Rob is dressed like his colleagues at the hospital: jeans, open shirt, Nike running shoes. No one here in the great southwest considers him underdressed, although such a getup at the hospital in Florida where I work would cause a stir.

The boy rubs his eyes as Rob lowers him to the floor with the command to walk toward his mother. On his tiptoes, he does.

"Is he okay, has he changed in any way?" Rob asks the mother.

"No, he seems all right," she says.

"Okay," says Rob. "His CT scan of the head shows a lot less fluid than before the shunt was placed, but I cannot tell if it'll build back up now. We'll need to keep him here and watch him and get another scan in the morning. He may not ever need another operation to fix the shunt or he may need one today."

The mother, a big-boned woman, handsome in part because she is watching over her son, seems to accept this astonishing ambiguity.

"So, we'll see," she says.

Rob and I were interns together 31 years ago. Rob was doing a year of general surgery en route to a neurosurgical residency and I was doing the same, planning to continue in general surgery. We hit it off, spent lots of off hours together and, although we've never again lived in the same state, we see each other two or three times a year and each time I like him and his wife, Ellyn, better. Rob is a serious and thoughtful man. He likes what he does—neurosurgical private practice. Contrary to common assumption, Rob's not getting rich and he works hard and those are just two of the reasons he's happy.

With deft and practiced ease, Rob has just wakened a sleeping four-year-old in an alien environment, examined his eyes, listened to his speech, felt the rigidity of his limbs, assessed his gait, and taken a careful historical account from the person who knows this boy better than anyone, his mother. He then explains the lack of certainty inherent in the boy's condition with such directness that the mother understands and accepts. There are no tears shed by mother or son.

I am gradually given to understand that in less than ten minutes I have witnessed a thorough neurological examination, a patient interview and a family conference. Over the next day I came to realize I was watching a pro. A pro at medicine, a long-ball hitter unheralded in Santa Fe: diagnosing, examining, operating, talking to patients and families, doing it right.

The next patient is a newborn infant with the same problem. His shunt was placed just yesterday as an emergency. Because the bones of the skull are still not fused together in the infant, the soft spot on top of the head (the fontanelle) is Rob's clue to diagnosis. No CT scan is needed here, because he can feel the soft spot and see if it is soft or distended.

It is soft.

The baby has several surgical staples in his scalp to hold the skin together and they are not pretty. There are twice as many as usual and they are irregularly placed.

"Hey Rob," I say "Why so many staples?"

"He kept leaking cerebrospinal fluid, so I kept putting in staples." He smiles. He knows the wound looks bad and he seems a little chagrined that I have brought this up. But he and I both know that what matters is that the fontanelle is soft and the child is not leaking spinal fluid. I'll bet he's seen lots of pretty scars that hide bad results. I know I have. I have one on my own neck.

The baby moves all fours (his arms and legs) appropriately and gives out a powerful yelp. It's a job well done despite the superficial appearance.

Down the hall and to the left an elderly man lies absolutely supine in a bed in a room with an eastern exposure. On his head he has a stockinet cap, made out of soft expandable bandage. His arms and legs are loosely pinioned by hospital restraints. I imagine that he is sometimes confused and might tear out his IV or climb out of bed and fall, hence the restraints. He has had a chronic subdural hematoma drained. A subdural hematoma is the collection of blood inside the skull, often caused by a blow to the head. As the blood occupies space, the brain retreats, pushed away by the collecting blood. There's only so much space inside the skull. Acutely, a "subdural" can push the brain and brainstem and the patient can die once the breathing center is compressed.

But Mr. Weathers has had his subdural collection for some time and it has gradually caused neurological symptoms. Two days ago Rob removed part of the skull and sucked out the offending old blood.

"Why do you keep him flat?" I ask.

"Well, these old guys need time for their brains to get used to all that space. If he sits up, that little brain might just slide down in his head." He smiles, shrugs, and with his palms up gives me a "what can you do?" look.

His last patient visit is an elderly woman who was treated years ago for a malignant brain tumor. First she had a brain operation, then radiation therapy. Now she is partially paralyzed and is difficult to arouse. She's not her-self anymore. Rob tells me that the tumor's cured but that her life is of little use. She's been injured by the "cure" to such an extent that she has no life. "She's got brain rot," he says.

I know what he means when he says "rot." There is no victory in the defeat of this brain tumor. The patient has been defeated, too. Rob spits out the word "rot." His ges-ture is one of frustration, irony and anger. This patient will live a long time without improvement and he is her doctor.

We walk out into the cold January sunlight and head for the squash courts. This is Rob's place, his beat. He has detected nothing extraordinary about the last hour. He has been doing it for years.

I'm quiet. I'm thinking if I ever need any kind of sur-gery, this is the kind of guy I want to do it. He's a profes-sional—thorough, competent, direct and talented. There is no artifice.

There are many days when I don't think about Rob, but I am always aware, somehow, of his commitment and skill. Antoine de Saint-Exupéry wrote about this sense of the distant, faithful comrade. In *Wind, Sand and Stars,* he wrote about young airmail pilots who flew from France to Spain and the Sahara:

> Round the table in the evening, at Casablanca, at Dakar, at Buenos Aires, we take up conversations interrupted by years of silence, we resume friendships to the accompaniment of buried memories. And then we are off again. Thus is the earth at once a desert and a paradise, rich in secret hidden gardens, gardens inaccessible, but to which the craft leads us ever back one day or another. Life may scatter us and keep us apart; it may prevent us very often from thinking of one another; but we know that our comrades are "out there"—where, one can

hardly say—they are silent, forgotten but deeply faithful. And when our path crosses theirs, they greet us with such manifest joy, shake us so gaily by the shoulders! Indeed, we are accustomed to the waiting.

I'm glad Rob and I had a year of training together, for I'd like to think I'm just like him. I love to shake him gaily by the shoulders. His hardworking presence reassures me that this profession and my choice of it are right. Many doctors feel besieged these days. They fear that their income is going to diminish, that their autonomy will be curtailed and that the quality of their lives is on the wane. After all that hard work and deferred enjoyment, it is all going to come crashing down around them. Things are going to change, that much is certain. But I can't help but feel that doctors like Rob will not suffer. Too much of their compensation comes in the form of satisfaction and pride of professionalism for any health care system to disrupt them. Yes, we'll make less money, but if we can just keep access to the patients and not have our hands tied too tightly in the management of those trusting patients, then it is going to be okay for me and Rob. You see, it is important to me for many reasons to know Rob is out there, doing it right.

6 Hanging

I don't care what they might tell you, any surgeon feels remorse and guilt when things turn out badly. Even if I have done the best I know how, a patient not prospering after a big operation takes over my life. In fact, I can say that each patient, from the time I make the incision until they are discharged from the hospital, fit and recovered, occupies a space at the back of my mind. I am on tenterhooks, sometimes more, sometimes less, about the outcome. Surgeons who tell you that once they have finished the operation, it's "up to God," are just suppressing their direct connection with the patient. Because I do cancer work, there is a special and difficult irony. Cancer usually doesn't hurt. There may be some bleeding or some weight loss or a lump, but for the most part it is not like appendicitis; the patient does not wake up at night twisted by sudden pain. So the cancer patient feels okay. Not great, but okay. Then I make the incision and then they hurt. They may know intellectually that they needed to be operated on, but they hurt more after I "help" them than before. I am always aware that mine is an act of controlled violence. And when there is unpredicted complication, or worse, death, it feels terrible. It feels like guilt and regret mixed together with a lonely isolation from everybody in the world who is not a surgeon with similar troubles.

Right now, I am sweating it out. I had planned the operation, discussed it with the patient, his family, and the residents. Then we did it. Things went well during the procedure. It was difficult, but I felt sure-handed and I had not had that fear that comes when I do not know if I can get it done or if I should even be trying to get it done. No; things went well in the operating room.

When an operation is smooth, when no undue blood is lost, when the case is done with dispatch and no fumbling about, then the postoperative period is usually straight-forward. I suspect that surgeons who refer to this situation as a "benign post-op course" have never been operated on themselves, because if they had, "benign" is one of the last words they would choose to describe the five to ten days in the hospital which follow a major operation. Although difficult and uncomfortable for the patient, the surgeon, who sees this all of the time, affects an attitude which is confident and reassuring: "This pain is normal, keep working on walking and doing your breathing exercises."

It is understandable that surgeons tend to spend re-markably little time with patients right after an operation. It is almost as if we do not want to see the physical and emotional agony we have caused. It is one thing to incise the chest of an anesthetized patient. It is quite another to see him gasp for breath, holding his incision, struggling to cough, while he looks at you with wide round eyes too polite and frightened to say: "What the hell have you done to me?" We all, I guess, want to keep our distance from that accusatory stare. So, if things are going well, the interaction is short.

Removed just a necessary bit, it feels not great but okay to reassure the hurting patient when the pain and soreness and fatigue appear within normal limits. Patients have a wide variety of responses to pain. Some are quite stoic and others less so. In time I have developed a sense about pain and I, like other physicians with a few years under their belts, now give more narcotics more liberally than I did as a righteous youth fearful of drug addiction and overdosage (both very uncommon in the average patient population).

But right now, something is not right. Each day I walk into Frank Mendez's room and we perform a 10-minute ritual: This 56-year-old man recovering from a colon cancer operation smiles wanly. "I think I am better," he says.

I note that there is no fever. His white blood cell count, a rise in which would signal infection, is normal. But the drainage from the tube in his stomach is high. Usually, as the intestinal tract begins to function after a colon resection, the amount of fluid drained from the stomach decreases as the gastric juice is propelled down the intestinal tract, and soon thereafter the patient passes gas and then stool. This function, (which society has us all tuck away with embarrassment) becomes the focus of the postoperative patient. They live to pass gas. It means the anastomosis, or hookup of the intestine, has healed. More directly important to the patient, it means the nasogastric tube can be removed. It means: I am better. I can get this damn tube out of my nose. I will make it.

I examine the wound. It looks okay. A little red, but not worrisome. I listen to his abdomen with a stethoscope. It is quiet in there. No sign of bowel activity. He is four days post-op. We should have some sign of bowel activity by now, but we do not.

"Your wound looks fine," I say.

Weak smiles.

"I am afraid the tube will have to stay in your stomach."

He looks away.

"It makes my nose and throat hurt," he says.

"I know," I say. "I will prescribe some local anesthetic to make it better." But I know it will not make the pain disappear altogether.

"Okay Doc," he says.

"It is a waiting game," I say, "Hang in there."

He and I both want the same thing. We want him healed, home, safe. He tries to please me. I try to please him. We are doing a bad job of it.

"Are you hungry?"

"No, sorry," he says.

Sorry? He is sorry he has let me down. But I feel I have failed him. He should be better by now. What is wrong?

The residents try to reassure me. "His x-rays are normal, no fever, white count is normal," they say. "Something is wrong," I say, "but there is nothing to do but wait."

And so we do, the patient, the residents and I. It is usually two or three days before things declare themselves, either get better or get worse. It is a long time.

At home, I am watching a PBS special about the singer Harry Chapin, but I am thinking about the drama unfolding on the fourth floor at the hospital. Chapin was so full of life until he was killed in an automobile accident. His sentimental songs are not liked by everyone, but everyone's heard them—especially "Cat's in the Cradle," a song about a man too busy to spend time with his son. The man then grows old and his son has no time for him. I am reminded of the three bright sons gathered around Mr. Mendez. What is wrong? Is there an abscess? Is there a leak where I sewed the cut ends of the intestine back together? Is there a collection of old blood sitting in the back of the abdomen? Is the blood supply to the intestine compromised? Should I get another x-ray? Of what? Going down to the radiology suite for an x-ray is so wearing for a patient. The residents, who sometimes order tests and x-rays with gay abandon, have no clue as to the tiring difficulty of getting out of bed, being wheeled downstairs, placed on a cold hard table for some x-rays "just to be sure."

I decide to wait. I am thinking of the problem almost constantly now. I find myself lost in conversation with my daughter. What did she say? I am thinking about x-rays and abscesses and re-operations. It is tempting to go to the phone and order an x-ray—let's do something.

That night I awake at 2:35 and then again at 4:30.

He has been taking steroids by mouth for arthritis. This treatment has relieved the patient's own adrenal glands from the stimulus to produce steroids. So during and after the operation we must supply the needed steroids to respond to the "insult" of an operation because his own glands are sleeping, anesthetized by long-standing steroid administration. Steroids are notorious for masking trouble. Excess steroid administration makes symptoms less obvious, tends to alter the white blood cell count, hides the clues of catastrophe. Maybe we are giving too much or too little! That's it! I call the resident at 5:00 A.M. only to learn that the dosages are appropriate. We may be obscuring important clinical findings with steroids, but at least we are doing it properly! I wonder if the doctor who initially prescribed these powerful drugs really felt they were necessary or if he just said to himself and the patient: "Oh well, let's try a little steroids." Did he ever guess what a problem these steroids might be?

The next morning I am getting squeezed from another direction. Tomorrow I am due to leave for a short holiday in Europe—seven days, actually. Now Frank is not worse, but he is definitely not better and, this late after the operation, that is definitely bad. I am supposed to leave tomorrow and he knows it. I go home restless.

It is late. I am packing and thinking. Is it hot in Spain? Is his anastomosis falling apart? What is it?

The airline calls. There has been a mixup: I cannot leave until the day after tomorrow. I am dejected, I am relieved. I've got one more day to see Frank get better or worse.

Next morning on rounds I am subdued. I am not going to Spain this afternoon. Now all the last-minute things I had to do have expanded to fill the time until the next day. Still, I am relieved.

Frank is absolutely unchanged. He is polite but weary. The wound looks good, his abdomen is not unusually tender (damn those steroids, are they hiding something?). No new clues. No improvement.

I go down to my office, sort through the mail, when the resident calls: "Mr. Mendez's eviscerated."

"What? I was just there."

"Well his small bowel is exposed." Frank's abdominal wound, the one I made transversely instead of up and down so it would be more secure, has split open and his intestines have spilled out onto his belly.

I am there in seconds. A fair amount of intestine is exposed. The muscle closure has fallen apart. The sutures are in place, but the muscle has just disintegrated around them. Were the sutures too tight, strangulating the muscle, making it die? It does not appear to be so. They are lying there, loose, in the midst of muscle the consistency of wet tissue paper. Steroids will do that.

Frank's eyes are wide. He reverts to his native Spanish. "*Tripes!*" he says.

Well, now we know.

"Frank, we need to take you back to the operating room, put you to sleep, take out the sutures, look in your abdomen to see if everything else is all right and close you back up with some big stainless-steel sutures."

"Okay Doc," he says. I think he is relieved, too. Or is it that me thinking that?

After he is asleep in the operating room, I cut the sutures and the abdomen falls open. There is no sign of healing—no strengthening of the wound, the dirty work of the steroids. The anastomosis of the intestine is intact. There is no abscess, no collection of blood, no compromise of the intestines' blood supply. The steroid-soaked muscles have not healed.

We irrigate the abdomen with warm saline. We are very gentle, lest we disrupt some other nonhealing tissue and make him worse. These are acts of surgical tenderness. I close the muscle, not in two layers this time, but in big bites, using stout stainless-steel suture so thick it is impossible to tie so we twist it together, like electricians. There are no subtle, gentle niceties about this abdominal closure. The thick steel will hurt later on; if the belly heals, it will stick and poke Frank. Much later we may have to take one or two out under local anesthesia. But I will settle for such trivial complications.

Will this closure heal? I do not know. If it does not, we are in big trouble—but for now it is about the best we can do.

After talking to Frank's family, I go home and pack. Yes, it is warm in Spain. I have no other distracting thoughts. Somehow I just feel he will be okay.

I am embarrassed. Frank's a prominent restaurant owner. He knows lots of people. They will all know I operated on him and he did not do well. Why is that an added cause of my concern? It is a public failure and it is an offense to my pride of craftsmanship.

I am relieved. I am hurt that he had a complication, but I was not on a plane over the Atlantic when he finally burst apart. And we knew what to do when that happened. I was here, I felt better and, I think, so did he.

Next morning before leaving I drive out to see Frank. He has the same tube in his nose and his belly's hurting but he has a big smile and he somehow knows the same thing I do: He's going to be fine.

7 Helping Sal— Knowing When to Quit

One of the hardest things I know is when to give up. Knowing when to give up on hopeless projects is the province of the truly gifted practitioner of any craft. There is a little poem or prayer that asks the Lord for the strength to know what can be changed, the serenity to accept what can't and the wisdom to tell the two apart. In surgery it is the same thing. There are decisions about which natural biological horrors to take on, about whether a tumor is resectable, about the patient's ability to withstand a big operation and her enthusiasm for it. I've gotten a lot better about these judgments, but sometimes I still miscalculate. There are times when I can't get the tumor out or the patient has a bad complication. Because things *usually* go well, these lapses in perfect result feel like a slap to my face and to my pride of craftsmanship. The patient, of course, does not care about how good my success rate is, she does not care about my professional pride; she cares about what happens to her. What happens is not always good. When things don't work out like we expect and a patient whom I think I can help is made worse by my efforts, it's a painful predicament, for I want to set things straight, make things better, start over again. Because it feels to me that I have *caused* the problem, I don't want to stop trying. I'm not talking about malpractice here, I'm talking about those

65

times when experience and carefulness and good intentions are impotent.

Once the patient and I have unknowingly taken on a losing cause, the dilemma becomes when to quit the fight. In time I have learned that it takes more guts to stop treating a patient when the prognosis shifts from grave to hopeless than to carry on doing what I know how to do. It is that subtle shift that is the secret. Patients don't declare themselves irretrievable, they just drift from salvageable to dying. I keep hoping things will get better, keep looking for treatable complications to fix. Then one day I walk into the intensive care unit and I just know it's over. In hindsight, patient's families are often angry that so much care was given before the end, but at the time, they usually push for more treatment. My consultant colleagues also want to keep on; they see only their part of the picture, the kidney infection, the heart arrhythmia. They don't step back and see that they are trying to fix the clutch on a car that has no engine. Only the wiser, older nurses approve when I start to prepare the family and patient as best I can for the end I see as ultimately inevitable, when even they, the patient and family, can't see the futility of further treatment. I have been here before and I know the territory better than they do and it is my responsibility to help them make out the shapes in the landscape that tell us all that the patient will die. It is just a question of how long and after how much treatment, or harassment, the end will come. This is not a skill you learn, then know surely for the rest of your career. It is always different and it is always hard. Sometimes the most important contribution I can make to someone's life is to help her see that it is over. I have never "assisted suicide," but I have helped patients disentangle themselves from the well-meaning but misguided machinery of medicine. And then they die.

Sal was insouciant from the start. She was in her early forties, but she had a tired look to her. She came over from a distant city, self-referred. She had no money or insurance, so it took a day or two of wrangling with the hospital to get her a bed. Sal worked as a waitress at a waterfront bar. She had a beautiful face, even though her skin was a sickly yellow-orange. She had become jaundiced a week ago. She didn't notice that the whites of her eyes had turned yellow, but the bartender did. Doctors in her hometown had correctly concluded that she had a cancer of her distal bile duct. The bile duct carries bile from the liver into the duodenum (the part of the intestine right after the stomach). En route it passes through the pancreas. To be cured (and these tumors can be cured) she would need a Whipple operation. This procedure is a big one. The bile duct and part of the pancreas and the duodenum are all removed and the remaining cut ends of all these organs are sutured back together in a complex way, so that the patient may eat again. I was not surprised that her doctors weren't interested in all this work on an unfunded patient. I am lucky. I work for a university and I get a salary. Although I'm sure my salary would be less if I did a lot fewer surgical procedures, I'm also sure it wouldn't go up much if I did more. Patients are billed for my services by the university. If the patient has no insurance, the university gets nothing. The university isn't losing money on me, so one of my perks is the privilege of operating on patients regardless of their finances. I would probably look at the situation differently if I were in private practice.

Sal had lived a fast life. She'd been married a few times, had a few kids, drifted down to Florida from Michigan. She had done some hard drinking and she had not yet licked her cocaine habit. She was tough. She did not look me in the eye. Her attitude seemed to be: "Yeah, yeah, yeah, what do you want?" I wasn't scared; I thought I could help her. Her initial x-rays suggested the tumor could be removed, so I scheduled her for a Whipple. She went home for the weekend. I had to fight with the business office to see that she could be readmitted. I promised she'd only be in the hospital a week or ten days. We sent her home with a "central line" in place. Her veins had been destroyed by drug use, so her doctors across the state had put a catheter into a main vein underneath the collarbone and threaded it into her superior vena cava, just above her heart. I left the catheter there, for I knew we'd have a hard time finding veins for IVs, too, and I didn't want to have to stick her again. It was an error on my part.

Sal was jittery the night she came back for admission. I explained the operation, its potential risks and possible complications, but she was clearly distracted. "Let's get it over with," she said. And so, the next morning, we did. It was the worst possible news: the tumor was stuck to a vein that carries all the blood from the intestines to the liver. The portal vein, it is called, and I have often thought it is the perfect metaphor for health, even life itself. The vein is plump and rich and full of life-giving nutrient-stocked blood. But the vein is thin-walled and can be treacherous when torn. Its fragile walls don't hold suture well and blood gushes out so fast you can't see where to sew and patients can bleed to death that way. Like health, the vein is robust and full but in an instant its injured thin walls can spill the life right out of the patient. Each time I taught one of my teenagers how to drive, I thought of the portal vein and how quickly their lives could be permanently changed or lost by a slight miscalculation at the wheel. They thought I was an old alarmist, just like the surgical residents do when I keep saying, "Be careful with the portal vein." Despite careful (very!) trying, I couldn't spring the cancer free of the vein.

To treat her jaundice, I bypassed the obstructed bile duct with small intestine, then biopsied her tumor to be sure we had the diagnosis right and closed. I told her mother she would live maybe a year or two, maybe six months. I knew I didn't know. The average is less than a year, but Sal was young and tough. The medical profession looks at survival this way: If a hundred patients have a certain cancer, how many will be alive five years from now? This approach comforts us and allows us to group our successes. But the patient wants to know: How am I going to do? Will I live? Medicine's inability to predict the outcome in each patient is the beginning of that patient's central disappointment in the doctor. It's an unsatisfactory business. I thought to give some definite news, so I told Sal's mother that the jaundice should clear within a week. When I went to talk to Sal, she wanted none of me. Staring straight ahead, she sneered, "You didn't get it done, did you?"

"You're right. I'm sorry," I said. I went on to try to tell her what had done and what I did know, but she waved me off.

Little did I know we were off on a horrible trip. The resident called that night, about 8:00, and said Sal was bleeding. Blood was collecting not only in the tube in her stomach, but in her abdomen as well. And her incision was oozing dark red, almost purple blood. The resident had run some tests and she had found that Sal's blood would not clot properly; something was making her bleed everywhere. There are two kinds of bleeding that occur after an operation. The most embarrassing to the surgeon is surgical bleeding. A silk tie comes off a blood vessel, some knot is not tied securely and blood collects in the abdomen or chest or cranium. Another operation is necessary. Although it doesn't happen very often, I hate this. The patient and family know something has gone wrong and they rightly hold me accountable. It means more pain, more risk, all because I did not do it right. On the other hand, surgical bleeding is understandable and it can be stopped. On those occasions when I have had to take patients back to the operating room, I feel bad right up to the moment when the patient is asleep and the surgical drapes have been placed. Then I feel better, because I know I can fix the problem.

The other type of bleeding after an operation is caused by a coagulopathy; the blood does not clot properly. This means that bleeding can occur anywhere and it cannot be stopped with sutures. Fresh blood products need to be given, the patient must be warm, and a cause must be found. Sal had a coagulopathy, and we did not know why. I drove back to the hospital, reviewed the situation, decided that reoperation would be of little hope and ordered transfusions of more blood clotting factors. Sal looked at me with "I told you so" written all over her.

I had not gotten into bed when the resident called again: Sal's temperature was 105. My God! After a simple palliative operation, this young woman was going to die! It was a long night. We cooled her down with aspirin and cold baths, started powerful antibiotics, gave blood and held on. By morning the bleeding had stopped and her temperature had come down. A routine lab test provided a clue. Sal had a high concentration of cocaine in her blood. Sometime just before her operation she had given herself the drug through the central line we had so "wisely" provided her. The drug infected the catheter and caused sepsis and she had damn near died.

Now her abdomen was full of old clotted blood and over the next several days this blood became infected by the bacteria that had coursed through her bloodstream and almost done her in. A week later she had an abscess, a high fever, and her lungs, affected by infection, could not support her oxygen needs, so we put the breathing tube back in. We changed her antibiotics, drained the abscess with a catheter and held on again. It took almost a week of knife-edge fear, but young tough Sal got better. Slowly. Finally she could breathe without the tube.

A month after her operation Sal was still in intensive care, the hospital accountants were all over me about sending her home, reminding me I had promised a week-long stay, and she still wasn't able to eat, so we had to feed her by that central vein. Each day, as we wrestled with one calamity after another, I had to keep reminding myself that this beautiful young woman had an underlying incurable malignancy! Her daughter came to visit. She was as beautiful as her mother. Sal's mother came down from Michigan. She said Sal was responsible for all her troubles because she "lived all wrong."

I don't think Sal came to like or trust or even grudgingly appreciate me, but I came to admire her. She was tough. She was nobody's fool. She fought like hell. We kept getting scans and finding new abscesses and draining them and she'd get better for a day or two and then worse again.

Six weeks after her operation, still in intensive care, Sal started to drain stool out her side and through her wound. One of the drainage catheters had eroded a hole in her intestine and stool was spilling into her abdomen and it was making her very sick. I was now forced to operate on this poor tortured woman. Whatever she had done in her short life, she did not deserve this.

Her operation was a mess. The best I could do was clean out the mess, put in big drains so stool would not collect inside her abdomen and hope. The medical student on the case decided surgery was out as a career for her. This was just too gross, too heartbreaking, too futile, too inhumane, too terrible. I agreed.

The nurses now knew that there was no hope of going home even for a while. There would be no time to "get her affairs in order." I knew it, too, but Sal did not. She was too young to have seen anybody "put their affairs in order." She did not know about saying goodbye. The nurses wanted me to write a DNR order. This excruciating document is a "do not resuscitate" order placed in the patient's chart to be sure that no futile, hopeless life-prolonging medicine will be given or action taken to delay the inevitable and prolong the agony. What used to be tacitly agreed to by the patient, her doctors and her family has now become a legal document. As such, it's a lot harder to do the right thing, because the order makes things so formal. Patients and families who would reasonably say "don't do anything heroic to keep me alive" now worry that by signing a DNR order they are signing a death warrant. Sal was in no mood for DNR orders, even though she was beginning to see the hopelessness of her plight.

We had a long talk one Thursday afternoon. I had just seen a clinic full of outpatients, some just getting over big operations, some just referred in for big operations, some back celebrating their long-term survival with me. I knew Sal was not going to be one of those.

"Sal," I said, "you look like you're having more trouble breathing."

"Yes," she nodded.

"Do you want the breathing tube put back in?"

"No," she said.

"Okay, I'll do what you want." That is as far as I dared to take the discussion. I had made some progress. Even though Sal wouldn't release us from the obligation to resuscitate her should her heart stop, she was being realistic about the breathing tube.

The infectious disease consultant was juggling several potent antibiotics in an effort to rid Sal of infection. I can still see John standing in the intensive care unit in his white coat, tall and healthy and young and handsome.

"We're going to change her drugs again," he said.

"Why?" I asked. "John, she has an incurable cancer, we've been torturing her for six weeks, let's give her a break."

Finally he agreed to stop the antibiotics. By now I was talking to Sal's mother and daughter several times daily, but I did not tell them why I had stopped the antibiotics. Was that deceitful? Should I have pressed Sal and her family to make the tough decision to stop these drugs? I don't think so and I don't think it is a matter of playing God. It felt like a matter of conscientious, thoughtful, moral, professional service. I knew there was no hope in a way that Sal and her family could not. I was healthy and experienced and motivated to help in a way with my ethical strength that I could not do with my hands. I hope to have the same service made available to me when I need it.

Sal appeared to have no other family or friends. So her daughter and I and the residents waited together. I kept hoping to get a call some night telling me it was over. But it did not come. Next day and next day, there she was, hanging on, testimony to my mistake and her strength.

One Sunday morning Sal died. By that time there was nothing left to resuscitate. I wondered then if I had quit on her too early or too late. When I think of her now, young as she was, I realize I was too late. I wish there were a way to tell her, her mother and her daughter. I'd still like to make it all better.

8 On the Table

It was a freak Friday accident, really. Another surgeon in an adjacent examining room had given a patient a mild sedative. The patient, a big, strapping 19-year-old, had become confused and combative. I heard the commotion and went to see. It looked as if he was about to fling himself out of the sixth-floor window. Careening from wall to wall, crazed, the boy struck the 60-year-old doctor. I tried to wrestle him to the ground. In time others arrived, the boy was subdued, and order restored. He was fine.

I do not remember being hit myself, but I felt bruised and I had a sharp pain between my shoulder blades. It hurt.

The next day, after a night of aspirin and no sleep, thinking I had strained a muscle, I called an orthopedic friend of mine. I went to his house that Saturday, and he confirmed the muscle pull and injected the muscle directly with Valium. I had not heard of this treatment before. It did not help. The next night was sleepless, too. The pain in the upper back was worse. I wondered if I would be able to work on Monday. Surgeons do not usually take time off for illness. It's not "manly." Given their common need to feel so vital, most surgeons show up at the hospital with the flu, broken bones and with all manner of cuts and bruises. They are not going to cave in to some mortal's ailment! But I wondered if I could operate feeling this bad.

I did, but I shouldn't have. I did a long case and that Monday night the pain was much worse. A muscle tear should be easing by now. What was wrong?

Tuesday, I didn't operate, I took it easy, I saw some patients, came home early, had a big glass of bourbon. But the pain was worse. Before going to bed, I went outside to put the top up on my wife's convertible. Getting out of the car in the dark, I didn't see the driver's window was up and I hit it with my forehead.

Startled, I extended my neck. Pain shot down my left arm. I was scared. Maybe I had neurological injury. Maybe it wasn't a muscle pull. Maybe my orthopedic friend and I had the wrong diagnosis. I said nothing and went to bed, but not to sleep. Wednesday I stayed at home, but did not get any better. Thursday I went to see a neurosurgeon.

I liked him immediately, in part because I wanted to. He was calm, careful, deliberate, slow to speak. I was reassured. After a physical exam he ordered some x-rays— routine views of the neck and a magnetic scan. The MRI, or magnetic resonance imaging scan, is a thing to behold.

I was placed, supine, in a narrow tube, like a torpedo tube, which was surrounded by a huge machine. No part of my body protruded from the tube. My arms were pinioned by my side. I could not move them. I could not bend my knees, I could not sit up, I could not see anything but shiny tube, inches from my eyes.

The technicians left the room, bolting the huge, heavy metal door behind them. And then the racket started, a loud banging noise. My nose itched and my back hurt. I had to move my legs, just bend my elbow, I had to get out. Despite the intercom, the staff could not hear me shout for rescue over the banging of the electromagnet. This must be what prisoners of war know. After 45 minutes of fear, panic, deep breathing, pain and more claustrophobia than I had ever imagined, a sweet young x-ray technician said she would like to get some more views, some different pictures and I said: "No!"

I was so relieved to be out of that torture chamber that it was minutes before I felt the pain again. My symptoms hadn't been helped by 45 minutes of rigidity in a tube. It was like being stuck in a sewer pipe.

The radiologist didn't look me in the eye when I had finished dressing. "I'll send the films right over to the neurosurgeon," he said.

Uh-oh.

The neurosurgeon said, "Your neck is broken and I think you have herniated a disc. I need to get a myelogram."

A myelogram. The myelogram is infamous. Fortunately, it is not used for diagnosis much anymore. A spinal tap is done and then spinal fluid is removed and replaced with a dye which, on x-ray, outlines the spinal cord. I could not imagine another test in this pain.

My ebullient radiology friend, Reed, I knew to be crazy. "No problem," he said, "We'll just inject the poison into your cord—hey, you never walked much anyway."

Well, I've heard enough black humor around hospitals to know that he thought he was helping me by speaking of the unspeakable, but rare, complication of the myelogram: paralysis. At that moment I learned about hospital jokes: They are not for the doctor to make to the patient but for the patient to make to the doctor. The patient is the one who needs the defense more than the physician. I have never forgotten this seemingly obvious lesson.

The myelogram is most famous for the headache that follows the procedure. It is called a spinal headache.

The spinal tap hurt a little. There were pins and needles down my left leg, but it was not too bad. And then Reed said: "Extend your neck. Tilt your head way back. I'm going to rotate the x-ray table so your head is down and your feet are up so the dye will slide down to your neck to show the problem area. But if you don't extend your neck, the dye will get into the skull and inflame the lining of the brain." He was describing meningitis.

Extending my neck was excruciating. The pain in my shoulder was sharp, central and severe. I thought I could not tolerate it another second. But to relax my neck's position would allow the dye to reach my head.

Reed continued to joke. He couldn't see my face and I couldn't summon the strength to call him off. I endured.

The myelogram confirmed the herniated disc and an operation was planned for the next day. I could hear Reed describe the findings to the neurosurgeon. I could hear him say, "Okay, I'll admit him now."

Being admitted to the same hospital I admitted other patients to gave me a view I had seen but had not understood before. I had been an inpatient when I had hepatitis in the past but I had not undergone an operation since I was a young child. I had passed by the admitting office a million times, seldom thinking what it must be like sitting in those plastic chairs waiting for the admitting clerk to pound my insurance number, my address, my weight and a hundred other seemingly unrelated facts into the computer. It's like standing at an airport in a foreign country, not speaking the language, waiting, trying to look polite and businesslike while the agent searches for your flight reservation. Only in a hospital you hope she *can't* find your name. Sitting there, I was aware of starting a process I could not control. Once I signed the admitting papers I could feel my ability to be in charge slip away. Maybe, I thought, one last time in vain, this pain wasn't that bad, maybe some physical therapy or injection would make it better. I was putting my neck on the line, literally. And I was entrusting these mortals, many of whom I knew, with me, my life, and the very movement of my hands and arms and legs. I was scared.

I inherited a wrist band with my name and my surgeon's typed on it. How many times had I held a patient's hand or wrist, looked down and seen "Dr. Karl" on it? There were times when the patient was shaking my hand, saying thanks, going home. There were times when the patient was sitting quietly, as I told him or her about their operation tomorrow. There were times when the patient was dying and I was holding on, just for a minute, to feel the loss for myself, to be sure. Now the wrist band said "Karl, Richard" and the doctor's name was not mine.

The nurses came in. First the real nurses. Then the administrative nurses. The former eyed me with some suspicion. They had had physician patients before and they knew what bad patients doctors can be. The latter were eager to please, to make a few brownie points. As the blood pressure cuff was inflated, I could feel my blood pressure going up with the column of mercury. I was on the lip of the waterfall and it looked like a long way down.

"Meet me at the back stairs," I told my wife, "and bring my pants and a shirt." I was going to escape. There was a great restaurant in Tampa that served the best grouper you ever tasted. After my surgeon came by to talk, I knew I had to escape. He had been careful and wary. I could tell he felt he had a well known colleague on his hands and it made him extra careful. He was direct: "You could be paralyzed from the neck down after the operation," he said. "I have to tell you that."

I hadn't had much time to pick my surgeon (note the possessive!). I was hurting and I was relatively new to the community. I didn't know whom to trust. I knew the new neurosurgeon at the university: arrogant, distant, slightly built with a beard, yet. Beards are distinctly uncommon among surgeons. They seem to convey an unsterile, un-washed look and are thought to be the mark of a sloppy thinker. I knew he felt he was great, but the arrogance made me wonder if he hadn't protested too much. (I have come to know him since and he is a good guy.) No, I'll opt for the reassuring, studious man who had graduated, I found out later, from one of the worst medical schools in the country.

He was, however, earnest and careful. I liked that. He wanted to involve an orthopedic surgeon; he planned to hammer a chip of bone taken from the pelvis into the space between the two neck vertebrae and fuse the broken neck. So a young, crisp orthopedic surgeon soon appeared.

"Aren't you Dick Karl's son?" he asked.

"Yes," I said. My father had been Chairman of the De-partment of Surgery at Dartmouth and this young man had done his general surgery internship there prior to his or-thopedic studies.

"Your dad's a terrific guy," he gushed.

"I know," I grimaced.

"Okay, great, after your operation, when he comes down to visit we can all have dinner."

"Great!"

It became clear the orthopedic surgeon had a vision of saving the bacon of his old chief's son. The man's eagerness to please the father had grave consequences for the son.

I did sneak out, eat lunch in a cervical collar brace and return to the hospital, paralyzed already by fear. But I was over the lip of the waterfall. The process had been set in motion and there was little chance of turning back. And it did hurt.

The night was excruciating. I lay on my back. The sheets tore loose from their hospital corner moorings and snarled hot calves while my arms wriggled to find some sort of comfortable position. It was no use.

I planned to place a strip of adhesive tape over my right hip at just the spot these two surgeons would be incising to take the bone graft. "Sam. Don't screw up," I wrote. When I think now of that desperate stab at humor, I shudder. What a poor, wretched, dependent, scared man taped that sign to his body. I am sure it did not help the surgeons either.

Dawn, finally. Stirrings on the floor. A nurse with an injection—sedative and atropine to dry up my airway secretions. I'm soon dry-mouthed and woozy, hung over and drunk at the same time.

It was different lying there looking up, familiar faces looming into range and then out again. They would say hi, good luck, then hurry away, my friends and acquaintances. I think now that they feared that they would be drawn in if they stayed. They thought they would somehow end up on the stretcher with me and then into the operating room and then onto the table. So they split.

I had told the anesthesiologist that I wanted minimum delay after I hit the operating room. "Put me to sleep right away," I had instructed.

But I hadn't counted on the time in the corridor outside the room. Lying there, my head was waist level to the nurses, surgeons and orderlies, waist high to my healthy self. I heard the banging of doors and instruments. Can delicate surgery be carried out by people who make so much noise? They slammed away, oblivious to one of their own, felled outside the operating room door.

"The suction is busted again."

"So he said he would think about it, but I haven't heard from him."

"That's the one with the big engine, isn't it?"

Would anyone ever rescue me? Finally it was into the room, onto the table.

"Hi, Dr. Karl," said Nancy.

"Hi."

"You'll be going to sleep now."

"Good."

What is this terrible taste? A disgusting sour, dirty, chemical smell clings to my breath, and my hip hurts.

I was in the recovery room. There was a styrofoam collar around my neck. I couldn't turn my head. Oh yes, I remembered, I must not turn my head.

My throat was so sore, and this smell and taste were awful, and my hip hurt.

"Okay, Dr. Karl, we're going up to your room," said my friend, a big orderly.

So soon? I've watched hundreds of patients in recovery rooms or PARs (post-anesthesia rooms). They're there for hours—waking, vomiting, voiding, getting their blood pressure checked. But I was being rushed out of here already.

I had no idea how unconscious those awake-looking patients are.

Well, I had survived, but I was not feeling very robust. I wanted to brush my teeth, but I couldn't move my head. I couldn't stand. The place where they took the bone graft from my hip, to "fuse the vertebrae in my neck," hurt. There was a branding iron in my side. And today, as I write this eight years later on a rainy Sunday morning, it still hurts.

I had to pee. The head nurse was there. And my wife. I couldn't go. All these ladies looking at my shriveled penis and I couldn't go.

"We'll have to catheterize you," said the nurse.

Oh great, I thought. My sore throat, neck and hip aren't enough; we'll catheterize him. It is said by psychiatrists that men experience an operation as castration, and I think they are right. I've never seen my genitalia look smaller.

"Leave me alone and I'll pee." I said. And then I finally could.

The incision, miraculously, didn't hurt. But my throat was too sore to swallow. By the next day, I could walk with hip pain, but I could not swallow. I was still on IVs and I still called every three hours for an injection of Demerol, which spread from the needle stick to a warm tide that washed from the center of me outwards, quietly relieving my pain.

There are lots of newer ways of giving pain medications now. There are the PCA pumps which allow a patient to deliver his or her own narcotic via an IV tube. By pushing a button a dose is delivered and the machine utters a soft "ding." If the patient pushes the button again, he will be rewarded with another ding—but if it's too soon, and an overdose might be given, no narcotic will be delivered. The machine records the frequency of button pushing and the patient's narcotic needs can be assessed and adjusted. But back then it was ring for the nurse, wait for the nurse, get the shot, wait for the warm tide. It was good to see the nurse and her needle.

The sense of exuberance which results from surviving the black tunnel of anesthesia and an operation soon gave way to more painful recognition. My throat was still sore three days later. I couldn't eat a thing—couldn't swallow the pills. I really didn't have enough incisional pain to warrant intramuscular narcotics, but I couldn't get the pain pills down. I oscillated back and forth between no pain medicine at all and the big-gun injectable narcotics. So I was either in pain or stoned.

I had surprising visitors. People I barely knew came by, brought a book, stayed for awhile. I had never noticed patients' visitors so keenly before this experience. Some patients have many visitors of the short-stay variety. The caller comes in, the patient feels obliged to be effusive, the caller jokes a bit and hightails it out of there. Others have close friends and family who virtually move in with the patient. They sit and read and nap, providing comfort just by their presence. I have concluded that this is the more sustaining arrangement.

Late on Saturday night a colleague in the Department of Surgery came to visit with his wife. They had been to a departmental affair and arrived in full dress with a thermos of my (usually) favorite beverage: martinis. But my throat was already on fire. My friend said: "The alcohol is a local anesthetic—it will numb the pain." So I took a sip. He was wrong. I coughed, gagged and gasped for breath.

The next day I was worse. My styrofoam collar, a two-piece affair secured around my neck with Velcro straps, began to stink. And my throat was not improved. I started to feel angry. Any survivor of an operation knows this: The patient is never as healthy again as he was before it all started. The operation may improve things dramatically but no restoration done with sharp knife and strong suture will approach the perfection of healthy youth. So, I'd just gone through this ordeal and it still hurt and I was not better and I wanted to see that son of a bitch who operated on me, the guy with the reassuring manner and the quiet voice.

Only he had gone on a cruise. His young partner came in. He was just filling in, he said, and oh yes, tomorrow he would not be here either; he was going to Jacksonville to pick up his new Porsche. I wanted to get my hands around *their* necks. There was no sign of the sycophantic orthopedist either. Remember this, surgeon: It's not just your hands and expertise and degrees and good looks a patient wants. This patient, all patients, want a human being who can look them in the eye, can comfort, can commiserate, can be honest and can, at the very least, be *there*. Goddamn it, I was angry.

Five days later, I went home. A cart carried the flowers and gifts and I dressed, leaving my top two shirt buttons open to accommodate my styrofoam collar. Home. The children, my own stuff. Home sweet home.

Although still hurting, especially my throat, I was driven to get out, go to work, drive the car. The need to reassure myself that I was alive (not castrated either) was powerful. The sore throat eased but there was still considerable pain in the back of the throat, and pain in my left arm and my thumbs were numb. Now that the smoke was starting to clear, I gradually became aware of a disagreeable possibility: Maybe this operation had not made me better.

I returned to my surgeon's office. He had his diplomas on the wall. He was tan from his cruise, solicitous. He was a little evasive. It's too early to tell what your outcome will be, he said. He ordered some x-rays of the neck. They showed everything was okay, he said. We'll see about the pain.

Well, we saw about the pain. It did not go away, but I wanted to ignore it. I went to work, I drove, I wanted to forget about it.

But it was there. And when I was tired, it was worse. I came to realize that I was not well, the same way a lover starts to recognize the end of a relationship. I wanted desperately to ignore the signs and symptoms, to deny the inevitable, to delay, to dispute the evidence. But just as certainly as an affair unravels, so I became conscious of my dread—this had all been for naught.

Another myelogram and MRI were ordered and endured. My radiologist friend wouldn't tell me what they showed. He sent the x-rays to the neurosurgeon and I followed, under separate cover.

"The bone chip inserted between the vertebrae, to fuse them, has slipped out. It's pushing on the back of your throat," he said, looking at my neck not my eyes.

"Someone said they had seen you dancing," he accused. Well, I had been dancing, all right. Nobody had said I shouldn't. But I know how he felt. He did what he thought was a good job on a colleague and it had not worked out and he did not understand why and it was easier to put it back on me, for dancing. I know now that he shouldn't have done that. I was hurting and he was strong. I needed his strength and he did not have it or could not give it.

We looked at the x-rays. The spinal cord was draped over the shifted vertebral bodies. The spinal canal had been narrowed, the bone chip had been spit out into the back of my throat and the whole mess had fused in this symptomatic configuration.

I left.

Over the next month there was little change. I went back to see the neurosurgeon. He was done with me. We could re-operate, he said, but he would have to put my head in a "halo." Screws would be driven into my head and attached to a ring around my head and attached to a support around my shoulders to see to it that my head did not move—a worse prison than the styrofoam collar—which by now, having been worn day and night, had a musty organic faintly rotting smell.

Right, I thought, I'd let you operate on me again. Fat chance. He made no return appointment.

Six months later I went to see two spine experts in Miami. One, a neurosurgeon, the other an orthopedist, disagreed about re-operation. One was for it, one was against it. I decided to live with it.

And so I did and the throat pain gradually got better as the bone was resorbed, and I got used to the faint numbness in my thumbs and the pain in my forearm is in my consciousness only sometimes now. But I am still angry and I see now why people sue their surgeons. They sue because of bad results—and for lack of eye contact.

About a year ago, the prospect of a ski trip came up and I decided to see a new spine expert who had moved to town. Was it safe to ski? I wondered.

I collected all of the old x-rays, reports and summaries. I liked this new fellow. He didn't spend long with me but he went right to the heart of the matter, looked at the films, then looked at me.

"Don't ski," he said.

"Look at these films from before your operation. The ligaments are torn, too. We would have treated you differently. We know not to try this operation. It's too unstable; when the ligaments are torn, the bone chip comes out and the whole thing falls apart."

We know now, I thought.

Did we know then?

9 Hotel Utah

I cut my finger in the operating room today. It wasn't that painful but I let out a pretty loud yelp when it happened. It made me shiver. We were just closing this man's chest after taking out his esophagus. It was one of those big needles used to approximate the ribs. They are about 3½ inches long with a pretty good curve to them. These days the greater pain is in the recognition of the risk, not in the actual piercing of the skin. Today's patient was a 63-year-old man with a cancer in his esophagus. We hadn't given him any blood and I don't think he's at any particular risk for HIV infection, but it's thought provoking, all the same. I was vaguely aware of a bleak scene of an old stone hotel on a gray wintry afternoon stirring in some back part of my mind.

I almost died of a needle stick once. I was just out of my residency and a new young faculty man at the University of Chicago. It was a glorious time of my life. I had moved to Chicago and set about discovering every one of its great restaurants and life as a real doctor. No more nights on call as a resident in the hospital, no more chronic fatigue, no more Marine Corps discipline. It was fun to be the surgeon.

As a recently trained young surgeon I was just a year ahead of the University of Chicago's chief residents and I wanted them to like me. After all, I knew much more about what it was like to be a resident than I did about being an attending surgeon, so at first I identified with them. One of the chiefs was a man from Argentina who had already trained at home and was now going through training again in the United States. (He has since become chairman of an important department of surgery in the northwest.) At that time, because of these circumstances, he had had more surgical experience than I, and that made our relationship a little odd for both of us. But he was and is a gracious and wise man with a good sense of fun and I liked him. I was helping him remove the colon of a pleasant lady from the north side of Chicago when he jabbed me with a needle. Back in those days, before HIV, needle sticks occurred all the time and we didn't think too much about them. He said he was sorry. I said not to worry. And that was that.

In February of that first year as an assistant professor of surgery, I went to the Society of University Surgeons meeting in Salt Lake City. The Society is a prestigious one and I was pleased to be invited because I hoped one day to apply for membership. Besides, I'd get a chance to see my friends from residency who had gone on to academic jobs at other institutions.

I checked into the old Hotel Utah with its high ornate ceilings and palpable sense of the historic intermountain west. You couldn't buy a drink in Salt Lake; you had to be member of a club to be served alcohol, so a group of us set out on a blustery cold and dark afternoon to find a club to join. We found an establishment in a basement that served beer only. That would have to do. I sat at a bar with friends from Sacramento and St. Louis and Chicago and ordered a tall cold glass of Coors. As my lips touched the glass, I had a shaking chill. I thought I'd picked up some virus and that I'd be sick for a few days. I excused myself, went back to the Hotel Utah and got into bed, pulling all the covers I could find around me. It was suddenly very cold.

I awoke to vomit. My roommate, a friend from St. Louis, slept on. I was grateful for that. I was embarrassed and wanted to be sick by myself. But through the night I became weaker and by daybreak I needed his assistance to get back into bed. The next day it became clear that something was really wrong; we just didn't know what it was. My friend bundled me up and put me on a plane and sent me back to Chicago, where it seemed even colder and darker. I was exhausted.

At home I went to bed and slept. The next morning, a Sunday, I called the chief resident, the man from Argentina, and asked him to come by the house and bring some intravenous fluids. I was sure I was feeling so lousy because I was dehydrated and that if I could just get some fluids in me, I'd be better. My wife, a physician herself, saw the folly in this plan. You need a doctor, she said, and she was right.

The next day my eyes turned yellow. Now we knew: I had hepatitis.

I was in the hospital for a week, supported by intravenous fluids, waiting. My liver function deteriorated daily and my blood chemistry levels got more and more worrisome. I was unable to eat and frightened beyond any previous fear.

"The last surgeon I treated for hepatitis, died," said the famous old gastroenterologist taking care of me. Of course, saying something like that wasn't giving me the feeling that I was being cared for.

"You're still very sick," he opined several days later after my liver started to recover. "You can't go home until you can eat a thousand calories a day."

I tried, but I could not eat without vomiting. I would take a swallow, then lie on my right side, figuring that maybe gravity would pull the food into the duodenum and out of my stomach before it all had a chance to come back up. It didn't work. With slow, exhausted and deliberate effort I started to hide the food from my tray. The staff soon discovered the discarded food in the wastebasket, but I found a place in the old bathroom, behind the mirror, where the cleaning people didn't look. My objective shifted from eating to *hiding* a thousand calories a day.

I was amazed and not reassured by how the hospital looked to me from the supine, resourceless position in which I found myself.. The nurses I had thought, as the attending surgeon, were the bright and able ones, turned out to be militant, gestapo-like tyrants. They would barrel into my room at 2 or 3 A.M. and wrap the blood pressure cuff tight around my arm, oblivious to the vast difficulty of falling asleep in a hospital bed while such peril lurked just outside the door. Nor had I known the gentle and positive effects of the nurses who empathized and took care with firm but always gentle understanding. They nursed. I had thought, when healthy, that these nurses were slow-witted because they did not know the patients' latest laboratory data and seemed so distracted by what I thought were vague and unimportant concerns. I did not know, until then, how hard it is to get well.

From that time on, I came to see the giving of care in a different way. It was my first real recognition that one must work with the nature of the patient and with the nature of the disease and the intersection of the two. It sounds trite and banal, but that illness and that hospitalization was a transforming experience for me. It separated me from the other physicians of my age. I had been sick and they had not. I was a young man, just 33.

After I got home, I still could not eat for weeks. I lost 30 pounds. But then, one night, after wrestling with a plate of

Swedish meatballs for dinner, and just after I had given up and retired to watch (more) television, suddenly I felt hungry. I got up, went into the kitchen, took the cold meatballs out of the refrigerator and devoured them. I ate and I ate and I gained the 30 pounds back in just a few weeks.

But I was changed. Simple daily matters became delectable experiences. The first time I drove a car after three months of illness was splendid. The color of the big stop sign was the richest red I'd ever seen. I got more out of living than I had before. But I wanted even more out of it. I began to question things more. I wanted more. I wanted more big operations to do. I wanted more nights out on the town. I wanted more friends. I wanted to be closer to them. I wanted a much closer relationship with my wife. I wanted a closer tie to myself.

The world around me, of course, had not changed. I looked the same once I got my weight back. People seemed to treat me as if I'd been on vacation. They didn't get it.

I had a better understanding of two things: I knew what it was like to be seriously ill and I knew how much I wanted a rich and connected life. And I knew I did not want to lose that life.

So a needle stick now calls up the fear of losing life and reminds me that I know how it happens. I have seen myself turn yellow, I know these things in a way that my colleagues don't. It is not an intellectual understanding. It is a visceral one.

My surgeon friends who do trauma work are the most exposed to HIV infection. Occasionally, when they are out of town, I'll take a turn at trauma call, so I have a little sense of what that's like. Not long ago we were operating on a young man who had been shot during an altercation. By the time I got to the operating room, his face was already obscured by the surgical drapes. He was in shock and there was no time for introductions. He had a big injury to his liver and he was bleeding very rapidly. We got some control of the bleeding and we were just regrouping to systematically remove the parts of his liver which could not survive when, about 2 A.M., a nurse stuck her head in the operating room door and said "John Doe's HIV-positive."

The chatter stopped. All I could hear was the suckers sucking and the sigh of the ventilator as it pushed oxygen into this man's lungs. Had I been stuck? Had any one else? These trauma cases are so chaotic—there's not the measured crescendo of an elective operation, where orderly steps are taken until the hard part comes and then the job is done and the anxiety dissipates and we turn on the radio and close the abdomen or chest. I couldn't remember anyone being stuck with a needle or knife, but now that information seemed so important.

We got out the protective safety glasses to prevent blood from splashing in our eyes (the residents call them "AIDS shades" to hide their fear) and we put on extra pairs of surgical gloves. But here's the thing: The knives and needles we use could pierce a hundred rubber gloves, so there's little solace in these paltry measures.

There is a sense of danger in the operating room now that wasn't there when I started in this business. We used to feel very aware of the possibility that the surgeon might harm the patient. We quoted the Hippocratic maxim almost daily: "First, do no harm." But now there's the uneasy recognition that the patient might harm us. There's the chance that a needle stick could infect the victim with a virus much deadlier than hepatitis. Now, I know that the number of documented infections of health care workers by such accidents is extremely low. But still, the current thought is that if you are stuck with a needle that has been used on an HIV infected patient the chances of becoming infected are one in two hundred and fifty. By comparison, the highest-risk heterosexual encounter, a female having unprotected sexual intercourse with an HIV-positive male, has a one in five hundred chance of contracting the infection.

We operated on this handsome young man four more times before he finally died of uncontrolled hemorrhage. I never did learn how he had contracted HIV; it just didn't seem to matter. I never learned if he was gay or if he had a drug problem. His parents, trim and clear-eyed, clearly cared deeply about their son. That seemed very important. We talked several times a day for those next five days. They were calm, but just. They understood the difficulties and complexities and they were always sure to express their thanks.

After many of these conversations I would take their son back to a cold green-tile room and re-explore his abdomen, trying, very carefully, to find tissue strong enough to hold a suture and to stop the bleeding. And I was aware, every minute, that that blood oozing out of his liver was carrying the virus.

I want to be careful not to overstate the anxiety. It's not incapacitating. But reassuring statistics are of very little comfort in the operating room. The very knowledge of the patient's infection changes the tempo and rhythms at the table. No matter how hard we try to act as if it doesn't matter, it does.

These feelings give me great pause to think about the history of brave medicine, about physicians treating the plague and cholera and yellow fever. Often, those attending the sick gave only supportive care, had no real way to cure and did not understand the disease at all. That part is just like today, really. But I've read about nowaday surgeons refusing to operate on AIDS patients and I have been ashamed of these representatives of my life's profession. How can these guys accept the high income and prestige and not accept the risk? It's like the army reservists who are incensed when their unit is called up. They are happy to accept the money and the PX privileges in peacetime but they object to the task for which they've been trained and paid. Those brave pros of medicine's past carried on and the enormity of their dedicated bravery is clearer to me now.

I admit to a certain relief when this young man finally died. I would not have to face the hesitancy in me to go back, one more time, to try to save him. I don't think I held back with him; I think I tried as hard to save his life as anyone's, but I was never unaware of his blood and his virus.

Now every time I'm in the operating room, I'm wary. I "double-glove" routinely. I worry about not just me hurting the patient, but the patient hurting me. It is more scary than it used to be. Tonight, on my fingertip, I can see a little red dot. It hurts just a little. In the back of my mind I can still feel the ornate lobby of the old Hotel Utah. It is cold, very cold. I rub my fingertip and wonder, just a little.

10 Midwest Bulletin Board

It was in the army that I first became aware of where patients came from. Until then they just seemed to show up at the hospital and the medical part of their story was so captivating that I don't remember ever wondering what their home was like or whether or not they had a cat. But working the night shift at the emergency room at the Fort Knox hospital forced me to see where the patients came from; I'd often see the wrecked car on the side of the road as I drove home. Once I was flown out to a crashed helicopter to see if there were any survivors (there weren't).

Sometimes a badly injured soldier would recover remarkably quickly and I'd have the sight of his wrecked vehicle still in the back of my mind. How could anybody survive in that mass of junk metal? It was the understanding of a patient as real that started the richness for me in surgery. It provides the context, it makes everything I do seem more important, more critical. I now know that patients and their families will spend hours dissecting a few minutes I have spent with them. "Did he say the cancer has spread?" "Was it the liver or the pancreas he meant?" And I now know how important it is to me that I know about the daughter in Atlanta, the one with the hearing problem; it fills me up with the place I occupy. I am at the center of something big and I have now the understanding of its extent. Why would anybody refer to a patient by a number? It robs the doctor as much as the patient.

97

I have been thinking about bulletin boards now, for about a week. I went past one at the hospital on Monday. It was in the pediatric outpatient area. There were lots of pictures of patients and families, but the one that caught my eye was a photograph of a 16-year-old boy, appearing the picture of health, standing in front of a small airplane with his arm wrapped around the spinner of the propeller. I like airplanes and I liked this young man's smile, but there wasn't anybody around who could tell me about the boy and his family and his disease and how he was doing. For all I know the picture is several years old and he is a college student now, or he may be dead.

But his picture reminded me of another bulletin board that I saw last summer, while I was visiting my brother in Sioux Falls, South Dakota. We had flown up there from Florida in my little airplane. The trip took all day, nine hours in the air dodging thunderstorms.

My brother is a specialist in pediatric surgery. He is two years younger than I am. On the morning after my arrival in Sioux Falls, a Saturday, I went with Steve to make his morning rounds and it was there that I saw a different, even more compelling, bulletin board. He was talking to the parents of an infant who came from a farm town over a hundred miles away. While he brought them up to date on their daughter's progress, I was left to fend for myself in the hall. Measuring three feet by five feet, this Sioux Falls bulletin board was jammed with what seemed like hundreds of pictures, all of young children. I guessed their ages ran from six months to six years. Although it was summer, many of the pictures had been taken at Christmas, with decorated trees and real snowmen in the background. At first I naively thought that these were pictures of the staff's children, posted to bring cheer to the nurses and doctors spending long nights in the hospital. But I knew almost in the next instant that these were pictures of the "graduates" of the neonatal intensive care unit. These were patients— babies who had brushed up against death almost before their lives had begun. These were pictures of babies who, with their parents and the staff, had fought off the devil and had won and gone home to prosper and be loved and to grow up acting like ordinary kids, who think life is no big deal.

I imagined that these pictures gave great solace to the parents of current patients as well as to the staff. How many mothers, waiting for the elevator to go get some coffee, had stood next to these snapshots and wondered if their own child would make it to the board? I know that some babies, no bigger than the size of your fist, will be in the neonatal intensive care units for months, struggling to get a foothold in this life. How many times had some baby's father paused to examine the cheery faces tacked up by the elevator?

Steve returned to show me the crucible whence these bewildered, brave young boys and girls had sprung. The neonatal intensive care unit (called the NICU or "nick-you" in most hospitals) at this hospital was a room about fifty by a hundred feet. Fluorescent light bathed the whole place, but there were many different local lighting arrangements scattered about the room. Some incubators had little hoods over them to shield out the light. Others had additional lamps placed just over them to treat babies with jaundice with light, which helps prevent brain damage. Incubators, radiant heat tables, cribs and bassinets were placed evenly throughout the room, close enough for one nurse to keep an eye on several babies, but far enough apart so that equipment, portable x-ray machines and rocking chairs had room for their functions; to treat and diagnose and to rock.

A nurse came over to speak to Steve about an infant he had operated on two days earlier. The baby, almost full-term, had been born with an incomplete esophagus, so that whenever the baby was fed, the feedings couldn't get down to the stomach, but spilled over into the lungs and caused coughing and then a pneumonia. In addition, there was a connection between the esophagus and the trachea, the breathing tube, which allowed the feedings to get directly into the lungs and made the injury to the lungs even worse. The baby was taken to the operating room and the connection between the esophagus and the trachea (the tracheo-esophageal fistula) was divided and the esophagus was connected to the stomach and the baby's pneumonia was getting better.

"Can we start to feed her?'" asked the nurse, a pleasant Midwestern-looking 30-year-old. She was businesslike but nice and I sensed she and Steve worked together often. There was no doctor-nurse formality and I think she called him by his first name.

"Sure," he said.

And with that one word he set in motion a lifetime of eating. With luck this young girl will eat every day for the next eighty years. She'll eat pizza and taste champagne and agonize over homework and worry about her own children someday, almost forgetting the fading scar on the side of her chest. The scar will be like a birthmark, for she will always think she was born with it; she will not remember the neonatal unit or the operation or the surgeon or the nurse. Instead she'll be told, on each birthday, how sick she had been as a baby and how we had all worried about her. The operation will become part of the family's folklore.

Steve is my younger brother and I hadn't ever really thought of him as this skilled before. But here it was: He could do something I couldn't. I'm glad for our sibling-rivalry days that I was 48 before I saw this evidence.

The most common diagnosis in the unit was prematurity. Babies without antenatal care, often of teenage, unwed, denying mothers, had been born too early and too small. Their lungs weren't ready to support them, they didn't feed well and they got infections. As Steve showed me around the room, I learned some sad facts. Only 40 percent of these babies had hope of going home to intact families with loving parents. Most were products of unplanned and unwanted pregnancies, born to child-mothers with few resources and little understanding of what was happening.

I asked him which babies were the most satisfying for him to treat. Of all the congenital anomalies, I wondered, which were the hardest to fix, which were the easiest? His answer as to the most satisfying surprised me.

"The ones with intact families," he said.

I asked what percentage of these kids had a chance of making it to the bulletin board.

"Oh," he said, "not very many. Most will survive, but the young mothers won't think to send a picture at Christmas time. Either they will have given the baby up for adoption, or had another child, or they move away, looking for a different life. Most of the children, maybe 80 to 90 percent, will survive, and an astonishing number of them will grow up healthy. But to get on the bulletin board you have to have a lot more than that."

I asked the nurse how many patients she looks after at a time. "It depends," she said. If the baby's real sick, it's one on one. At most, if the babies are 'growers and feeders,' I'll care for four or five." One on one, I thought. Imagine.

We looked around some more. Steve showed me a child who had been born with no abdominal wall; the intestines and liver were just hanging out of the baby. Steve had constructed a covering for the intestines and the baby seemed to have no other abnormalities, so the outlook was great.

"These babies are fun to take care of," he said. "The surgery is quite straightforward and the families know something terrible is wrong and that an operation is essential. It's not like you're trying to explain some hidden, vague but lethal, internal defect. They get it."

After Steve cleared up a few routine questions, we walked out to the elevators. He met a colleague and we were introduced and then Steve and his friend had a chat about another baby and I found myself in front of the bulletin board again.

I thought about a teacher of mine—one of the best, most riveting, most demanding teachers I'd ever had. Her name is Jessie Ternberg and she was a pediatric surgeon at the Barnes Hospital, Washington University in St. Louis. That is where I learned the trade. From Jessie I learned strength and straightforwardness. I learned not to treat babies like little adults. I learned that a mother's well-being was almost as important as the baby's. I learned (again) never to take things for granted. I learned that this slight pretty blonde woman could hurt me. She had exacting standards and she was not about to be seduced by some fast-talking resident who might be a little full of himself and not yet instructed about the difficulties of tough surgery and the price paid for error or inattention. She would point her pianist's index finger at me, scolding me for a minor misjudgment about taking out stitches or feeding a baby too soon. That finger would whack me on the chest and it wasn't until I got home that I'd notice the pink-red welts earned working for Dr. Ternberg.

Jessie Ternberg had fought her way into pediatric surgery in the fifties, when there were few women surgeons and no pediatric surgical training programs. I remember being told of the hazing she got from the men. They made her sit outside the surgeons' dressing room while they got dressed. Jessie had to dress in the nurses' locker room. Some faculty members fought her appointment to the staff when she finished her residency. Millions of offenses, great and small, hardened Dr. Ternberg's assessment of her fellow surgeons but it did not dilute her great warmth and care for her patients. To this day, if I spend an extra minute with a patient's daughter or mother, it is human skill I learned from Jessie Ternberg.

I never really knew if she liked me or not, but I sure wanted her to. After I had left my training and was a young assistant professor of surgery at another Midwestern university, I got a great boost from Jessie Ternberg. The department of surgery had lost its pediatric surgeon, so the general surgeons were pitching in. This made the pediatricians very nervous. They knew that we had not been trained specially in pediatric surgery and they distrusted our abilities. The surgery department chairman wanted us to do the pediatric surgery: He did not want to admit there was a hole in the lineup of his team.

I got caught in this crossfire one day when I was asked to see a patient born with a missing diaphragm. The neonatologist said the baby should be transferred to another hospital. The chairman of surgery told me to do the case. I was in a terrible bind. If I demurred, the chairman would label his new faculty member a wimp; I'd be ridiculed by the others; my whole career could be marked by this loss of resolve. But, I thought, was I up to this? I had only participated in a few such operations. There was an experienced pediatric surgical team in the same city. And the neonatologist was going nuts: Transfer the baby, he said.

I called Jessie Ternberg. "What should I do? You know the operation, you know me and my abilities, you understand the politics." She said: "Do the case. And tell that goddamn neonatologist that you're not worried about the operation, but whether or not *he* can handle the kid post-op." Then she hung up.

And so I did the operation. And the baby did fine. I had earned my spurs and, yes, growing up in surgery is like that. Many cases over many years in many operating rooms have verified Dr. Ternberg's message: Believe you can do it. If you don't believe you can do it, you'll never be able to do it. Does this sound arrogant? I am sure that it can. I remember very clearly how frightened I was about that case. I remember being frightened for the baby and myself. But somehow, sometime, a surgeon must take those first few steps that make him or her the one for the job. Jessie had given me the last shove out of the nest. She knew the risks. Had that baby not done well, I wonder what I'd being doing today and what I'd be like.

Now, standing back in front of the bulletin board, I had a much greater respect for the pictures than I had had an hour earlier. I understood that getting well in the neonatal intensive care unit was only part of the task, and the easier part at that. Some of the babies, those whose pictures were not pinned to the board, had been discharged to a life even harder than that which they had first experienced, fighting for their life in the hospital. Now they would have to fight for love, too.

The pictures were even more arresting now. I saw three-year-olds with cows and pigs, six-year-olds with bicycles and younger brothers. I saw some beautiful smiles.

And as you read this, there is a nurse in Sioux Falls, leaning over a baby who weighs a pound. She is picking him up right now, tucking him in the crook of her arm and offering him his first meal. When I go back next summer to see Steve, I hope I see that baby's picture on the bulletin board.

11 Retirement Party

I am sure I went into surgery because of my father, who was a surgeon. It isn't one of those pretty stories of a young boy hanging around with his patient tutoring father, though. We didn't talk about what he did so much as I was given to understand that what he did was very important and very serious.

When I was ten or twelve he'd come home late—usually after nine—and have a drink. My mother, who had saved dinner for him and had not eaten herself so that she could join him, would bring the food out to a coffee table in the living room and my brother and I would drift out there too, to join him, for he was big. Big in every sense. He was tall and handsome and alive and the air in the whole house changed when he arrived. I'd ask what he had done that day and he would tell me without sentiment which operations he had done. He'd then get down to the assignments I had been given: to split firewood or look up something in the encyclopedia. I was drawn to him and the exciting life he went off to, but I was also aware that he was measuring me and not often pleased by the measurements.

By the time I was in high school, I was more skilled at avoiding him. It seemed I had never done quite enough to earn his praise and just seeing him ran the risk of another assignment. Twenty years would pass before I would come to love him for those assignments. They gave me strength and taught me perseverance. Back then, though, his tasks seemed pointless and mean. I wanted to play baseball and see friends and it seemed as if there was always something I was supposed to be doing around the house.

And there were the residents. Dad was working in a teaching hospital and he was surrounded by young men (exclusively men, in those days), aged 26 to 34, who were learning surgery. He had several he had picked out, become a "father" to and would bring to the house. When I was 15, a resident of 28 was a scary thing. The resident would be married and have had a hugely successful college and medical school career and own a car. All things I wanted desperately to do but had not done yet. Some had built their own telescope or rebuilt their car engine. Had I done anything that wonderful lately? No, I hadn't. And if I didn't get to work, I never would. I came to loathe those residents, always coming around, delighting my father, showing me up as an incompetent teenager. It was as if they were the sons he really deserved.

So, as I got older and went to college and then medical school, I was gearing up to take those guys on, show my father I was as good as they were. But when I became a surgical resident, my father's new surrogate sons became photographers and businessmen, so I could not go head-to-head with them on the surgical testing ground. What I did instead was to seek out my own surrogate fathers to mentor and approve of me. They were famous surgeons, some even more famous than my father and, later, newspapermen and lawyer-politicians and corporate presidents. I'd lovingly tell my father of the exploits of these men and of their obvious approval of me. I guess I was trying to say: Hey, these guys think I'm cool and you should, too.

Then when Dad retired, I went to a dinner his colleagues gave for him. I was going to see those residents from years ago. I was going to learn about those relation-ships from the perspective of a grown man. I was going to learn about where he had been all day before he got home, tired and noisy and demanding, around nine o'clock at night to sit down to dinner at a marble-topped coffee table with my mom.

There he was, the guest of honor, all six foot three of him, turned out in an elegant blue suit, vest and pocket watch. He stooped some, the better to hear the well-wishers who had gathered at the elegant old Hanover Inn as the sun set over the glory of the Vermont countryside and the ripple of the Connecticut River. It had been the first really warm weekend of the spring and the buds had responded—they were that shrill green. Many of the guests had the hint of the year's first sunburn earned while un-covering their rose beds to see what had survived the New England winter. The sun shot through the none-too-clean windows of the formal receiving room where the drinks were served, and I caught a glimpse, often, of sun hitting him full-face, making him blink. Other times it just glanced off his full head of hair as white as Robert Frost's but fuller, thicker. He is a big man, strong torso and wide hands, sort of what Robert Frost would have looked like if he had had Studs Terkel's more middle-American elemental stuff.

There had always been a little of each, Frost and Terkel, in my father. Part poet, part workman, he was retiring, after 50 years in medicine, two stints in the Navy and four very different hospital jobs. For 40 of those years he had loved being a surgeon as few do.

The guests were surgery department colleagues, old res-idents now out in practice or at the medical school still, for-mer secretaries—and his children, two boys (my brother and I are both surgeons) and a girl (a lawyer) and eight grandchildren. After the drinks we retired to a private dining room upstairs.

What a crowd! Mostly surgeons, a few internal medicine men, a urologist or two, and the stately old gastroenterologist who had been chairman of the medicine department when my father had been chairman of surgery. He, the medicine chairman, had recruited him, the surgery chairman, to New England for they had been blood brothers at Cornell, where they had led, respectively, the medicine and surgery services at Bellevue in New York, the biggest city's biggest city hospital. They knew about indigents and human neglect and the lowest forms of life and the most noble, all of which they had learned, together, at that city hospital, the St. Elsewhere of them all, Bellevue. They, the medicine chairman and the surgery chairman, had come at their own pace and in that order to New Hampshire to fashion a four-year medical school out of a two-year prep school—Dartmouth.

There were many stories abroad in the room. Old resident mates greeted and postured and swapped tales; wives told of growing children and life in Ohio, Texas, Alaska.

In time, the chicken florentine cleared, the succeeding chairman of Dartmouth's Surgery Department presented the honoree with an 1847 edition of William Beaumont's volume about his experiments in the stomach of Alexis St. Martin, the voyager injured by a musket blast which laid his side and stomach open to Beaumont's curious view. It was a beautiful volume about modern medicine's beginnings at investigation just over 150 years ago. Beaumont's observations are famous in American medicine, as they were among the first made outside of Europe. With St.

Martin's stomach open to the skin, Beaumont had nursed St. Martin back to health while watching the digestive process first-hand. He placed various foodstuffs into the stomach and noted their fate. He also noted that the cathartic given to St. Martin and taken by mouth soon poured out of the side of the patient. There is some question about the Beaumont–St. Martin relationship, for it seems the patient was not allowed to go after he had recuperated; rather, he was prisoner to Beaumont for three years, while the doctor worked at getting famous.

Soon, the tall and elegant former chairman of medicine stood to get the record straight about his retiring surgeon counterpart. Understand that medicine types and surgical types traditionally hold each other in mutual mock disdain. The surgeons feel that internists think to the point of paralysis, mentally flogging the patient's laboratory results with analysis that produces more confusion than result. Internists feel that surgeons act without thinking, that they are always so eager to cut that a patient can be entrusted to a surgeon only *after* an operation has become unavoidable and the decision has been made. "Don't tell the surgeons about this patient," they will sometimes say, "we have to save him from the cowboy cutters." Depending on the hospital, this natural antipathy can range from eye-twinkling amusement to downright mean contention.

"When Dick and I were young," he said, " the internists indulged themselves in a parlor game of surgeon baiting. They taunted the surgeons, claiming these mindless technicians operated on the 'when in doubt, cut it out' school of surgical sophistication.

"About this time we were just learning about allergy and allergic shock. Children dying of a bee sting or patients dying from a penicillin allergy were still mysteries. Sudden death from an allergic reaction [when complete cardiovascular collapse and death may bring down a healthy human being in less than a minute—called anaphylaxis] was among the most feared developments.

"One day Dick was removing a mole from the chest wall of a prominent colleague. After he injected the local anesthetic, the patient grasped his neck, then collapsed into shock. Almost by reflex, Dick quickly cut out the entire area—removing the site of the allergic reaction—leaving him with a large hole in his side (which was later skin-grafted) and saving his life. Dick told us later he had thought about what to do. He had anticipated this catastrophe. But I can tell you that the 'when in doubt, cut it out' aphorism disappeared from our hospital for a while!"

Generous laughter greeted this story and I looked around the room, wondering about the surgeons there—some just beginning, some about ready for their own gold watch. I paid special attention to their eyes. People often think they can learn about a surgeon by examining his hands, and maybe they can. But I look into their eyes. It's there that I learn more about care and safety, intensity and will, courage and experience. Old good surgeons seem to stand up straight and they'll look you in the eye. In fact, they seem eager to look you in the eye.

I saw some eyes that had seen some things. I imagined many of the guests standing in front of an x-ray view box at 4:00 A.M., rubbing those tired eyes, trying to make sense of the x-rays six inches in front of them. There was laughter and fraternity in these eyes now; this was a club meeting and the group started to come together. Yes, we're surgeons, what a great story. I would have done the same thing, damn right! The men sat straighter, their wives looked at them, these visiting strangers who come home late at night or leave early or can never be counted on to be there for the dinner party. So this is where they go when they go away!

The floodgates had opened. Everyone sprang up in turn, attacking the rostrum to tell his or her own story. There were some women surgeons there. They seemed accepted and part of things, not tokens or outsiders with their noses pressed to the glass of the operating room windows. They belonged. Stories of tough cases, difficult patients, a wonderful vignette about our hero up to his elbows in bleeding but knowing he had things under control, turning to a young medical student in the throes of making a career decision between medicine and surgery (and who probably did *not* know things were under control), and saying, "Sure beats pushin' pills, doesn't it?!"

In one corner sat an elderly, stately man, slow of motion with an elegant white mustache. Next to him perched a younger man, maybe 40, compact and trim with deep dark eyes, intense and coiled. And what a pair they made!

It seems the older man, a retired vascular surgeon, had, almost a year before, suddenly developed excruciating pain between his shoulder blades. He knew at once what it was. He knew his aorta, the main artery leaving the heart which carries blood everywhere, had developed a leak, or "dissection," so that blood was burrowing into the wall of his aorta and dissecting away its layers, like peeling off the top half of a napoleon pastry, leaving fewer layers of artery to contain the blood pumped out of the heart under high pressure. He knew he would die if his aorta was not repaired immediately, before it burst.

His wife rushed him to the emergency room. His years of surgical command helped him overcome the inertia that exists in any medical emergency. The hard part, often, is recognizing that the situation *is* an emergency.

"I'm Dr. William Rogers and I have a dissecting aortic aneurysm—get the surgeons," he told the medical intern.

The intern looked at him with an "I'll be the judge of that" condescension. "Look, I'm not kidding, get Phil Lee." Lee, the newly recruited cardiac surgeon, paid heed. He took him straight to the operating room; he knew Rogers to be a good diagnostician. He put him on heart bypass using the heart-lung machine, opened his aorta and sewed a new dacron graft in place. Paraplegia and death are the two most common complications of a dissecting aortic aneurysm even when it is successfully repaired. In fact, the chance of Rogers's surviving back then had been at best only one in five.

But there he was, drinking his after dinner coffee and sitting up straight. Right next to him, eyes alight with the evening's celebration, sat Phil Lee. These two surgeons knew each other in an entirely different way. I looked at both of them and at their hands and into their eyes. Both knew how it feels in the hands when the tissues will not hold sutures, when the body is so weak and ruined that no surgeon can help. They had both seen bleeding. Both had felt that horrible pit in their stomach when the bleeding is so fast you can hear it—wet like a brook—and you do not know if you can stop it. And there they sat, the savior and the saved, both knowing how close it had been. You could see it in their eyes, imagine it in their hands.

I did not know if I'd be called upon to speak. I did not know if I wanted to or not. I started out just playing it safe, thinking up something to say if asked, without distracting from the real business of the night. But as time went by, I became more earnest in my effort. As I sat witnessing the tributes, I picked out three defining characteristics of this surgeon father that I admired. I began to see how his strengths as a father were not unrelated to the tributes now cascading down upon him as a surgeon. So I thought of these components of real character:

First was his seeming lack of fear. That gave me confidence. No matter how great the challenge or task, he always used his mind and strength to give things a try. One time his new color television didn't work and so he took the back off, ignoring all those "caution do not remove, high voltage" placards. He did not know a lot about color television but he knew basic electronics and, by God, more often than not he found an answer, a cold tube or a loose wire that he *could* fix, and what pride and satisfaction he took from that. No fear.

Perspective was another quality. I remembered a time he had invited me for dinner when I was in medical school. "Can't come," I said, "I have to memorize the cranial nerves." There are twelve cranial nerves and they *are* complicated. The first cranial nerve is the olfactory nerve and it carries the information about smell to the brain. The second cranial nerve is the optic nerve and carries visual signals. Think for a minute how extraordinary and discriminating these two senses are—and these are only the first two cranial nerves! Cranial nerves 3, 4 and 6 control the movement of the eye. They innervate various muscles, called the extraocular muscles, to do the job. You can diagnose a cranial nerve deficit by asking the patient to follow your finger with his eyes, an ancient secret of physical diagnosis. That's only if you have memorized these nerves, where they go and what muscles, exactly, they control. The fifth nerve moves the facial muscles. It has three branches and a complex anatomical course. And so on.

"Oh, they're not hard," my father said. "One allows you to smell, you see with two. Three, four and six move the eyeballs around, and five makes you smile. Come for dinner." And so I did and learned about perspective.

The third trait I wanted to tell everybody about was persistence. I remember a patient whose femoral artery (the artery to the leg) had been repaired and the site had become infected and the sutures tore loose and he bled. And this surgeon of tonight's affection took him to the operating room and took out the infected sutures and repaired the artery again and gave antibiotics and hoped for the best, which did not come about. He bled again. And again the surgeon repaired it. Again it failed. Over and over at ten-day intervals they fought, the patient and the surgeon, to save the man's leg. And in the end the sutures held and he healed. Lesser men would have tired and given up and lost, but not this surgeon and not this patient. Persistence.

But it became clear to me that this was not my night to share these thoughts, for I had not known the man as the others present had. I was not one of his residents and I had not known him as a colleague. I did not go to medical school with him, had not shared call with him. I had never operated with him. We never had adjacent lockers in the surgeon's dressing room. But I realized even more as I sat there listening to the praise of his students and peers, how much sustenance I took from knowing that he was out there—seeing patients, doing difficult cases, worrying about the infection and the bleeding, teaching, learning, standing for the right thing, succeeding mostly, failing sometimes too.

But I was not part of the group so I held my tongue. I had my own special relationship with him so I thought

I would tell him these little examples in private, though I knew how much he'd be embarrassed. Through his assignments and chores my father had passed on down to me these very gifts. It is a lucky man who feels driven to grow up to be like his father when his father is so big in goodness, humor, and strength.

12 Match Day

The fourth-year medical students are getting anxious. It's getting close to match day. In a few weeks they will find out where they're going to spend the next several years of training. This spring, after they graduate, most will pack up and move to another city and another institution to start their internship on July 1. Some will stay here, of course, but even so, the friendships of the past four years are about to undergo the same disassembly that high school students discover when they finally go off to college.

The fourth-year students are pretty worldly now. They are kings of the hill. They have mastered this medical school business and because they learn so much so fast, they know a whole lot more than the third-year students who are themselves miles ahead of the second-year class. Last fall each fourth-year student trekked off to other medical school hospitals with the training programs they sought: surgery, medicine, ophthalmology, obstetrics and gynecology, orthopedic surgery and so on. They drove or flew, stayed at inexpensive hotels near the big hospitals and tried to guess what it would be like to be a resident at that place. Were the residents happy? Did they get enough responsibility? Was the call schedule too arduous? What was the clinical caseload volume like?

Each student underwent a battery of interviews with attending faculty. At some places these interviews are quite exacting: The faculty ask the students specific questions about medicine. Out of context, away from the home

117

medical school, this type of questioning can be frightening. Some institutions think it is a good way to learn about the applicant's grace under pressure. I think it's just intimidation and that there's still too much hazing going on in medical schools these days, even though it is a lot less than it used to be.

I guess we interview about 120 students during the fall on four or five separate days. Each student is interviewed by at least two faculty members. This is a fascinating window into the development of a young doctor. Somewhere between that first year of medical school and that last year of residency, the character of a physician is determined. Almost all the students are, at first, altruistic and very excited about medicine, real medicine. But sadly, I can't make that same statement about all the finishing residents. Somewhere along the line, greed and hubris and this astonishing sense of entitlement can infect some of them. I still don't know how to detect these future traitors with any great reliability. That's why I say I'm such a bad interviewer: I can't tell the hardworking, compassionate, thorough and knowledgeable from the poseurs. I've taken to asking about the nonmedical interests of each applicant. Some have little to say; they want to do medicine because they want to "help people" and they "enjoy science." And just when I conclude that these must be the fakers, I remember that I probably couldn't have done much better thirty-five years ago and I believe I have it in my bones now, so I cut them some slack.

In early January we have a departmental ritual: We gather at 6 P.M. in a very plain conference room, eat potato chips and drink soda and "do the ranking." That means we list in order of our preference the students we hope to recruit to our residency program. About the same time each student fills out a ranking sheet, listing the programs he or she wants, in order of preference. A big computer in Illinois matches the applicants' wish lists with the programs' wish lists so that if the applicant's first-choice program has ranked him highly, he'll get that internship.

Popular programs may have six jobs to offer and they may be filled by that program's top 12–15 choices. Less popular institutions may have to go as low as the 35–40 ranked candidates before all the jobs are assigned. Some programs "don't fill"; some positions go begging.

At most medical schools most students land a position that they have ranked as one of their top five or six choices, but some students "don't match."

On a Monday in March the teaching programs and the medical schools find out whether their programs have filled and if any medical students have failed to match. If either has happened, the next 48 hours are frantic: Programs look nationwide for next year's interns, while deans of students search for jobs for those students left out in the cold.

Our marathon ranking meetings are fun. We rarely get together like this as a group and most of the surgeons have quick wits and we are all, after all, off the record here. Sometimes the ranking session reveals more about the faculty than it does about the candidates. One associate professor of surgery will say: "He's a great guy; he'll work like hell and do just what you tell him to." About the same individual another faculty member will say: "He's slow-witted and dull. He's gotten through medical school on sheer perseverance. He's never had an original thought in his life."

There are some generally agreed upon criteria we look for, though. Membership in Alpha Omega Alpha (AOA), the medical school honor society equivalent to Phi Beta Kappa, is held in high regard, at least most times. Surgeons admire a capacity for work and a sense of passion about surgery; these traits validate what they like about themselves. They don't like applicants whose primary concerns seem to be the night call schedule and the amount of free time they are likely to enjoy. They do like the fourth-year student who wants to know when he'll get to do his first operation. Enthusiasm is important. An uncomplicated disposition and, in truth, an athletic sense about the applicant is important.

In most surgical training programs only 10 to 15 percent of the applicants are women. The long training period and the difficult hours are partly responsible for this phenomenon. Residual reluctance of mostly male faculties to accommodate training programs to the needs of young women in their childbearing years is another explanation.

Despite all the care we take in the selection process, I am continually astounded at our collective inability to consistently pick winners. And, as I said, I am worse than my colleagues! Often a good intern fails to mature into a good chief resident. Hard workers, they never seem to be able to give up the compulsive need to manage the small things in a patient's care so that they can concentrate on the big picture: plan for the patient's operation and rehabilitation, see to the family's questions and fears. Others cannot take the grind; they get quiet and six months later go into radiology or emergency medicine.

One young man, from a good medical school, proved up to the work; he has the passion, he has the intellect. He grew and got serious, joked less, read more. His operative skills blossomed and he seemed destined for great and full career. But when I see him sporadically now, it's clear he's not happy. He's got a huge practice, has written several good papers in the literature, but he can't seem to enjoy it. I don't know why and I never would have guessed.

On that Wednesday in March when the matched students find out where they are going, there is a party. It starts about noon. The gaiety in the room is fueled by anxiety as each student waits to hear where he'll be on July 1.

I remember my own worries on that day almost thirty years ago: I wanted to go to a Harvard hospital and I hoped for the Massachusetts General. The "Mass General" was the most prestigious surgical internship I could think of. But my interview there had been lackluster and I thought it more likely that I'd end up at Case Western Reserve in Cleveland. Even today, I can remember how it seemed so damned important. I wanted my medical school mates to see how good I was by being chosen by a good place. The reputation was, I am afraid to say, more important to me than the educational content of the program. I listed Washington University in St. Louis as my last choice, even below my safety school in Rochester. I had been to St. Louis for an interview, saw nothing distinctive about the Barnes Hospital there, and concluded that it was a long way from my New York City roots. I almost didn't list it at all. Besides, very few of my peers had ever heard of the place.

When that Wednesday arrived, I was tired from so many sleepless nights, irritable at the possibility that I might be embarrassed by having to admit to an internship in Cleveland or Rochester. I had small, but real, hope for Boston.

I got Washington University. I was devastated. I slunk from the medical school party, locked myself in my room. I thought perhaps I'd do a year of research, wait it out, apply again next year, a wiser and more experienced intern applicant. I spoke to almost no one for several days. I asked a nonmedical friend where St. Louis was. He said he did not know. I asked him: "If people in Indiana are Hoosiers, what are those in Missouri?"

"Losiers," he replied.

In the end I had no real choice and I went to St. Louis with a big chip on my shoulder, angry and arrogant about my Ivy League pedigree, now soiled by this unknown Midwest unprestigious place. I need to tell you this, though: I soon learned that the quality of individuals and the medicine they practiced in St. Louis was far better than New York, the University of Chicago, or any other place I have been, before or since. The combination of Midwest straight-ahead, let's-get-the-job-done, no-nonsense mentality and the sheer brightness of the people at Washington University made and makes for a very powerful, very wonderful mix. And today I think Washington University has the best medical center in the land. This New York snob learned a lot there. A lot about medicine and strength and courage and compassion and healing. Not one day goes by when I do not put into play something I learned from my last-choice institution.

I have hanging in my office a beautiful needlepoint, made for me one year by a delightful fourth-year medical student named Joyce. Joyce had taken an elective in her last year of medical school. It was a one-month rotation on the surgical service at the cancer center. I got to know her over the first few days of that stint: She was aggressive and questioning and interested. I already knew that she had decided not to go into surgery, so I was perplexed that she took a surgical "clerkship." That experience is usually so difficult that only prospective surgeons ever do it. But

Joyce had a thing about surgery and, although she had decided on pediatrics, she was treating herself to one last total immersion in surgery. Joyce had great surgical aptitude, the part you cannot teach but is either there or it isn't. She had a sense about handling human tissues and a sense about handling human emotions, a rare combination.

During her month with us, she got sick. She developed a tumor in her pituitary gland that caused an increased secretion of prolactin, the hormone responsible for stimulating the breast to produce milk. Although the tumor is benign, its location in the center of the brain is of strategic importance. If the tumor gets big, it can impinge on the optic nerves and cause loss of vision to the right and to the left, so-called "tunnel vision." And, of course, there was that eerie milk production. Her response as a young woman to this information was remarkable: Joyce did not hide the fact that she was seriously ill, that she was frightened, and that she had to excuse herself during the day for diagnosis and treatment (the treatment is medication and it is usually successful in arresting the growth of the tumor). On the other hand, she did not wallow in her disease and did not use it as an excuse to withdraw from her assigned clinical duties. In other words, she demonstrated that rarest of qualities: honesty about a difficult situation and the grace to deal with it with a minimum of fuss and denial. She was inspiring.

Right after New Year's, Joyce came to me to ask me to write her a letter of recommendation. I was flattered. Joyce had scored in the top 10 percent of her class for all four years, was a member of the medical school's AOA chapter, had great skills as a doctor and great strength as a human being. She wanted to go to Duke University to train in

pediatrics and then do pediatric endocrinology, a specialty
no doubt of interest in part because of her own illness.

"Joyce," I said, "I'll be glad to write you a letter. In fact,
I'll write you two."

"Why?" she asked.

"Well," I said, "you are a first-rate student at a not well
known state medical school. So you won't be treated as if
you're number two in the class at Harvard. Secondly, lots
and lots of kids want to go to Duke; it has one of the best
pediatric training programs in the world. We need a way
for you to stick out, to catch their attention. I think the
grace and dignity and strength you displayed when you
were sick were very telling about your qualifications as a
potential pediatric resident. So I'll write one letter which
describes these strengths and how I got to see them in you.
I know that'll be an invasion of your privacy, so I'll also
write a letter of praise with the description of your illness
edited out. You can pick which one you want me to send."

Joyce chose to send the longer letter. As match day
approached, she came by several times. Once, she brought
cookies and admitted sheepishly that she was just trying to
appease the gods of internship (what pull she thought I had
with these gods, I still don't know). On the morning of
match day she arrived with a framed needlepoint of a
quote from Sir Berkeley Moynihan. On a white background, in large black letters, it said:

Surgery . . . after all, is an affair of the spirit; it is a fierce test
of a man's technical skill, sometimes, but, in a grim or long
fight, it is above all a trial of the spirit; and there are few
things that can not be conquered if a man's heart is set on
victory.

Wow.

I didn't know what to say. I was pleased and surprised. No student had ever done anything this grand before. She had made this for me. I was also a little worried: I knew Duke was a long shot, that she might have to console herself with a good program somewhere else and that it was really a crapshoot at her level. How had the professors at Duke taken my letter? I didn't know.

"We find out at 11 A.M.," she said. "I'll come right over and let you know."

"Good luck. It's not all that important, really," I said lamely.

Just then the phone rang and somebody had just perforated his esophagus and needed an emergency operation. The burst esophagus had contaminated the left chest and the patient, a man in his fifties, was pretty sick. We put him to sleep, rolled him left-side up, prepped and draped his left chest and entered the thorax through the bed of the sixth rib. We found the hole, closed it and put a buttress of muscle over the closure. I didn't think to think of Joyce and her career at all.

After the case, I went out to talk to the patient's wife. She had a million questions and was clearly angry at one of her husband's doctors whom she held responsible for the perforation. I was tired. It was about 8:30 P.M. when I finally got free, walked to the changing room, put on my "street clothes," and snuck down the back stairs to my office.

There were about eight or ten phone messages on pink "WHILE YOU WERE OUT" slips; calls from some patients, from some friends, from one of the kids, from the dean, from the car place about the part on backorder. There was no word about Joyce. I looked at the new needlepoint, propped up on the back of wingback chair in the corner of the office. I'm tired, I thought, I'll find out in the morning.

I went to call home and tell them I was on my way, but not to hold dinner. And there, on the back of the phone, was pasted one of those Post-it yellow sticky message slips. On it I saw just four letters in a big loopy scrawl: D U K E.

As I got in my car, I switched on the headlights and thought: Another match done. I wonder how our other students did. Did they get the jobs they wanted? Did they all match? Did our surgery program get the people we wanted? Did we list the best people first, or were we fooled?

And then I thought about Joyce and I remember thinking this: She was lucky to get Duke; it is a very good program. And Duke was damn lucky to get her; she is going to make one hell of doctor. It *was* a good match.

13 The Norwich Classic Car Rally

This whole business about health care in this country has gotten beyond the breaking point. In clinic today I saw a young man who could not have been more than 45. He had had a rectal cancer at age 38. He'd been operated on, then received chemotherapy, then radiation. Now the tumor has recurred. He's been left impotent by the surgery or the radiation, I don't know which. About six months ago the auto dealership where he worked went under and now he has no insurance. He and his wife of 19 years have about $25,000 worth of assets—well above the cutoff for receiving some sort of social funding program.

So here is a guy with an unimaginably bad hand of life's cards: His cancer is back, he's unable to pay for further care (which in itself is very unlikely to help him much, but it might) and he can't enjoy a sexual relationship with his wife, whom, I was convinced during our short meeting, he loves. And, I think, she loves him.

While I looked at the x-rays, his wife sat pensively at his side. When we talked, they were comfortable with each other, not interrupting one another as warring couples often do. I could tell that they had been over all this a million times. They were planning to divorce.

That way she could have the car and the boat and he would be destitute and eligible for some sort of funding.

Here was a couple who, against today's odds, still loved each other after 19 years and they were brought to the thought of divorce to find a way to afford treatment that has a small chance of working. There was no sign of the doctors or hospitals who had treated him when he had insurance money. He was now at the state-supported cancer center, essentially begging for care.

It has seemed reasonable to me for some time that we must find a different way of allocating our medical resources. This same week we read about twins joined at the chest being separated at a Philadelphia hospital at astronomical cost. The parents were aware of the horrible abnormalities of their babies at 13 weeks of gestation, but their mother decided to carry them to term. The father has admitted taking funds donated for the operation and using the money to buy cocaine. For a long time it has seemed very clear to me that we can't afford this type of care when we don't do the simple things, like get the mammogram to detect breast cancer at an early stage, when it can be cured.

But. But.

I no longer have that smug understanding. A trip to England changed my mind from righteous clarity to ambivalent uncertainty.

Michael had been calling for weeks. The Norwich classic car rally was to be held over a weekend in the end of May. Michael, an old college roommate and a friend for 30 years, needed another driver for one of his painstakingly restored 1954 Jaguar Mark IIs. Besides, Rob and Ellyn, friends of mine from Santa Fe, would be there, too. Rob and I had been interns together in 1970 and friends ever since. You've met him before. When Rob and Ellyn went off to England for a year in the late 70s, I gave them Michael's name and so Michael and his wife Gina had become friends with my friends. Now we could all be together in the English countryside, driving two beautiful old cars through ancient country lanes. It seemed too good to miss.

It all fell into place. The airlines were having a fare war. A friend said he'd be glad to cover the surgical service for me. The kids all had someplace else they wanted to be over the long Memorial Day weekend. There was room to stay at Michael's friends' house in Shipdam. And so, I figured, why not?

Rob and Michael drove down to Gatwick airport to pick me up. Even after flying all night, I was exhilarated to see them. We went to the flat that Rob and Ellyn had rented in London for their holiday. We went to lunch at the pub, we drove to Michael's, we talked to Gina. Finally at 4 in the afternoon, or 11 in the morning east coast time, I was allowed two short hours of sleep before we all started off for the rally. We set out with Michael and Gina, each of whom had brought another friend, and me and Rob and Ellyn. We drove out of London on a Friday evening, just joining the last urban escapees to the country. Michael and his old schoolmate, David, drove the first Jag. Gina and her old friend, Barbara, followed in the second restored cream-colored white Mark II. At the rear came the Americans, Rob and Ellyn and me, in the "sweep car," the modern-day Ford thought reliable enough to go get parts should either of the Jags break down.

Rob is, as you know, a neurosurgeon in Santa Fe and I have held him in high regard since our internship days together. His quiet thoughtfulness is beautifully balanced by the exuberant warmth of his wife Ellyn. I was pleased to half-doze in the back seat as we set out.

But the rich farmland and the green fields and blue, backlit sky of this May evening soon roused me wide awake. It was beautiful as we caravaned northeastward toward East Anglia with the sunset behind us. I was now sitting upright, leaning forward between the two front seats, locked in conversation with Rob and Ellyn, like a thousand other times in many other places.

It was a little strange, this righthand-drive Ford, with Ellyn sitting on the left, not driving. But the company was familiar and the friendship unlike the kind one makes in middle age. These were old, old friends, in this car and in the two Jaguars ahead of us.

In time the conversation got around to the choices of health care. Rob and I are among the very few surgeons that I know who voted for Bill Clinton, and neither of us was all that happy that we had to. I know I did primarily to get the health care coverage issue off the dime.

"What do your fellow docs think in Santa Fe?" I asked Rob. He's in private practice and I knew that his perspective might be different from that of my colleagues, cloistered in academics.

"They're scared to death," he said. "They think that health care reform will hurt their incomes and hurt the quality of care they give."

We talked about the few outrageous specialties where ophthalmologists or heart surgeons make millions. We also talked about hardworking pediatricians who are lucky to make $80,000 a year. We talked about how American medicine had gotten greedy and not looked after the population they way it should have.

We agreed that liver transplants, heart transplants, pancreas transplants for diabetes, and bone marrow transplants for all sorts of cancers were expensive and probably not worth the money. At least not worth the money when there are 37 million uninsured Americans who get very little care until they're shot or collapse and are rushed to some emergency room where even the accountants don't have the heart to kick them out of the system. Not worth the money when we can't do the simple things: get mammograms to detect breast cancer at an early stage, when it can be cured; can't screen for cervix cancer; can't vaccinate our children.

Rob and Ellyn had thought about these things. So had I. And we agreed we had to save money at the high end so that we could buy the simple effective things at the low end.

By now the sun was low in the sky behind us and we had turned off the M4 and were throttling along straight but none-too-wide old English roads, hedgerows on each side, the tail lights of the preceding Jags sliding around in our windshield. The hedgerows gave great reverberation to the exhaust of the old cars, a deep throaty sound as if the Jaguars were ex-smokers.

The roads narrowed even more. We were close now. Our hosts for the weekend were a couple in the advertising business and they had done well. They owned a seven-bedroom, four-bathroom house in the country near Shipdam. A house of that size in the U.S. is a big spread; in the U.K. it's a mansion.

Both the wife and the husband had been married before. Each had had a son in a previous marriage. And each boy was living with them now. That still left plenty of room for me and David in one room, Rob and Ellyn in another, Michael and Gina in another and Barbara in yet another. There was even room for another couple driving up from London as well.

A turn onto a gravel road told us we'd soon be there.

The Low Farm was just that, tucked behind a low hillock, and it had so many outbuildings that at first I couldn't tell what was house, what was garage, and what was converted barn. We parked in a gravel space enclosed by buildings. The Jags were switched off almost reluctantly. It was dark now and cold. I was bushed.

We tumbled into the mud room just outside the kitchen, our excited breaths leaving little bits of fog in the air. A dog greeted us, a cat scurried away, and then our hosts opened the kitchen door and we fell into the warmth of the kitchen.

The kitchen was the first room of the house to be built. It was at least 300 years old. It had a very low ceiling and exposed old beams of hard wood and a rough plank floor. Rob and I had to duck to clear the beams. The counter space was the latest German high-tech, as were the dishwasher, refrigerator, and stove. They all gleamed white. The warm room easily accommodated all the travelers and hosts. For me, it felt great, like taking off boots after a long hike.

Much hugging and introducing ensued. As usual, I missed most of the names, even though I had been practicing on the trip up. Specifically, I couldn't sort out the two sons. Both were robust-looking boys, one about 19, the other about 22. Finally Simon, the older, more muscular one with blond hair in a ponytail and thickrimmed Michael Caine glasses, said:

"Doctor Dick! I've heard so much about you, it's grand to finally meet you."

It's funny, but I never think that my friends have an English accent; they are my friends and what they say is what hits my ears, not the clip to their dialect. But when Simon spoke, I finally realized, almost 24 hours after I left Atlanta, that I was in England. Simon sounded very British.

"You must be exhausted," he said. "By my calculation you've been up for two days running and still on the go.

May I offer you a spot of tea, a glass of wine, or a proper drink?"

"Oh, a proper drink, please," I said. I mean what difference would it make? I was neither awake nor asleep; neither tired nor rested—just lagged.

"Right, then. Would a single-malt scotch do you?"

"Oh, yes, of course, thank you"

"Would you like it with ice and water, or the English way, neat?" he asked

"I'll have it neat, thanks, as long as I can get a glass of ice water to go with it."

I took a long draught of water and an equally healthy sip of scotch. Wow! It was strong and good and thick and smooth. Fatigue suffused my every capillary. I looked around the room to see lots more hugging and three or four animated conversations swirling around this old-new kitchen. I was the only new one in the group. So I was feeling that my conversation with one of the sons was sort of banal compared to the catching up with one another that was going on. But I was about to relearn the lesson that life is never uninteresting; you've just got to pay attention.

"Doctor Dick," Simon asked, "would you allow me to join you?" The formality was endearing.

"Of course!" I say.

"I'm learning to drink from my younger stepbrother, Stewart, here."

Stewart then emerged from the gaggle by the kitchen fireplace and slapped his brother-by-vagary playfully in the shoulder.

"I'm teaching him to screw the girls, too," said Stewart. He was obviously earthier than Simon.

"Simon," I asked, " where have you been? Why are you learning these pleasures from this younger man? I'd have thought you'd be teaching him a thing or two."

"Oh," said Simon, "I couldn't think of any of this until I had the heart-lung transplant."

"The what!?"

"You know, a heart-lung transplant. They take it all out and put a new set in. I couldn't get out of my room without the portable oxygen and all the tubes. It wasn't conducive to drinking or screwing."

I'd lost my balance now. I'd been up for two days on the run, I'd just driven for three hours while wrapped in talk of health care reform, I'd just finished a man-sized scotch and now the young man in charge of refilling my glass was telling me that he was alive because he had successfully undergone the surgical tour de force of a combined heart and lung transplant—one of the very operations we'd all agreed just a few hours ago to be too expensive for any society to bear. I was looking at an exuberant 22-year-old man whom I had just condemned to death by virtue of withholding a transplant. I was very grateful I wasn't in charge of health care in Great Britain, or any where else, for that matter.

He poured me another scotch and I woke up to learn more about him and a little bit more about myself. Simon had cystic fibrosis, a disease that causes thick lung secretions and recurrent lung infections, ultimately destroying the lungs. Sometimes the heart weakens from having to force blood through the diseased lungs. Heart-lung transplants have been used successfully in these patients, both in Europe and in the United States. Improved immunosuppressive medicines which protect against organ rejection have made these procedures more successful. But they cost hundreds of thousands of dollars.

"How were you brave enough to undergo such an operation?" I asked him.

"Oh," he said, "it's not a question of bravery. I mean, one can go down the road of transplant or down the road of no transplant. I've had cystic friends who said no. They just didn't want to go through it all."

"What happened to them?"

"They're dead," he said, matter of factly. "But it's not bravery that made me do it."

I decided to take another tack. After all, he was only 22.

"Okay. What then is the bravest thing you've ever done?"

"Oh," he said without hesitation, "get in the car and go to the hospital."

"My mother was away and I was here alone and I had no way to get to the hospital and I didn't know what to do when the bleeper went off and they told me they had a transplant match for me. So I organized a cab because I had to get operated on within six hours and the hospital is three hours from here. So I left word for me mum and off I went. But it was hard deciding to get in the cab. I wanted to go back upstairs and get into bed. But I was too winded to make it. It was just easier to get in the car.

"Once I got to the hospital they shaved me and took me in and put me to sleep before my parents got there."

"Did it hurt when you woke up?"

"Of course it hurt, but the funny thing was, I woke up with a tube in my trachea and five chest drains and I knew right away that I could breathe for the first time in ten years. It hurt, but it was a great hurt." He pronounced trachea as "traykeeah." He served us each another scotch.

Still reeling from this discovery in East Anglia, I pressed on about his mother's feelings during all this. I could see the others in the room separating into two groups: Those who knew the story already carried on with their conversations (they were even a little annoyed; there goes Simon with that damn transplant saga again, how can we compete with that?); the others, new to the tale, clamped onto our group. It is true that as extraordinary as his story was, he had to get on with his life, and an event like that can knock everything out of perspective.

Simon had gotten on with it. He'd gotten a job installing car stereo systems. He had some money now, and some friends. He had plans for later tonight. He and Stewart were going into town for Saturday night. They both seemed to view Simon's employment in recession-cloaked England with as much astonishment as his heart-lung transplant.

I went to bed, but could not get the story out of my head. What had his mother felt? (She had arrived at the hospital while the operation was in progress. She and the boy's father had gone out to a pub. She said they had shared an intimate time with each other that was a relief from their divorce strife. She had the look of a woman who had been through an experience that could neither be told nor described. She looked relieved to be worrying about the lunch plans for tomorrow's rally.)

What was it like to do an operation like that? How empty the chest must have looked when both lungs and the heart were removed. There must have been a great sense of wanting to get the replacement organs sewn in place as quickly as possible. The thoracic cage must have looked very vacant after the lung-heart bird had flown.

How could any of us understand how grand a thing this was? How could any society possibly withhold a remedy this magnificent from any 22-year-old boy confined to bed with oxygen? How would we ever pay for it all? But wasn't it better than price supports for tobacco? Or billions for "star wars"?

Over the next few days we did some beautiful driving and we did some splendid eating and we had some wonderful conversations. Simon came in and out of our midst with the easy grace of a young man with lots of things to do and places to go.

Just when the whole thing was too big to comprehend, the English sense of humor rescued us all.

At lunch Simon said, "My stepfather complains that because the donor of my heart and lungs was Irish, all I want to do is eat potatoes!"

The rally finished at Silverstone, the grand old Formula One racing track north of London. I got the prize assignment: drive one of the Jags back to London as the sun set. There was lots of hugging and talk about next year's rally.

As we all got into our cars to head off in opposite directions, Michael turned to Simon and said to him:

"Take care of yourselves."

14 Luck

It's been a long time since I found out about the surprising lack of correlation between a surgical job well done and a smooth, successful postoperative recovery. I remember as a resident, even, noticing that sometimes a beautiful operation performed by one of my heroes, one of the best, would end in bad result; either a major complication, or a major complication and death. On the other hand, I saw some none-too-well executed operations conclude with happy patients and what I thought was undeserved praise for their less-than-expert surgeons. What could explain this incongruity, this breach of the moral connection between effort and result? Well, I still don't know and it still happens—not often, but frequently enough to make me think. I have not been an overly lucky surgeon, one who can relax and still get good results. I still feel that I have to try as hard as I can and that if I don't, the patient and I will suffer. Even at what feels like full effort, bad things happen and I feel responsible. Then, too, every once in a while, I (and the patient) get very lucky. It is pleasing when that happens, but I feel a little guilty about it. Two patients tell this story themselves, Jonathan Tims and Reggie Richards.

Jonathan Tims was betrayed from within. He was a fit 51-year-old oil company executive with a perfectly functioning body except for one organ: his intestine. For ten years Tims had argued with his colon, the lining of which kept leaving him in torrents of diarrhea. He had learned to accommodate to the symptoms of sudden and cataclysmic rectal bleeding, weakness and fluid loss. He had heard, really heard, the admonition of his doctor, who told him that his disease, ulcerative colitis, held more than troublesome symptoms in store; his diagnosis was associated with a prohibitively high incidence of cancer. Finally, Jon consented to an operation to remove his colon. He eschewed a complicated operation which would reconstruct his anus and leave him with a normal, albeit frequent, way to go to the bathroom. He chose a simpler operation that would leave him with an ileostomy—a "bag."

Jon had been admitted to the hospital last summer for the operation, but his debilitated state required a few weeks of intravenous feedings, "hyperalimentation," to build him up for the operation. To do that, a catheter was inserted through his neck into a "central vein"—in fact, the vein which drains directly into the heart: the superior vena cava. But last summer, complications set in. The catheter became infected and Jon developed a high fever and other obvious signs of infection. The catheter was removed, but the fevers continued. The infection had jumped off the catheter and taken hold somewhere in Jon's body. Ultimately the site was discovered. Jon's heart valves harbored the infection. Little seeds of bacteria clung to his valves as they opened and closed 84 times a minute. You could hear the murmur with a stethoscope. Six weeks of intravenous antibiotics were prescribed and Jon consented. He wanted to rid his heart valve leaflets of the second Trojan horse. First his colon, now his heart was the enemy inside him.

In time the infection was corralled and, miraculously, Tims's colon symptoms abated coincidentally, as if he had been compensated for his heart's misfortune. Jonathan Tims was discharged and went home, chastened by his own frailty and that of his heart and colon.

In late fall, Jon's symptoms became worse. Despite his memories of last summer, he agreed to be admitted for his overdue operation.

When I first met him, Jonathan Tims was the picture of a confident businessman momentarily sidetracked into the hospital. He asked pertinent questions and was very cordial. But in his affect now there was a hint of fear, for Jonathan had learned things last summer about the slender thread of health. He knew about fragility. He knew about bad luck.

"Jon," I said, "I will remove the entire colon and rectum; your bottom will be sewn shut. I'll bring your small intestine out to the skin, where it will empty into a bag."

"It's strange," he said, "how the colon can be so sick and yet the contiguous small intestine is free of disease."

I talked to his beautiful wife. She agreed with the plan. "I just want him well," she said.

Two days later, at 7:30 A.M., we met again, Jon asleep, supine, pinioned on the operating table, me scrubbed, gowned and gloved. The incision was midline, from the breastbone to the pubis. Examination of the abdomen was routine. The colon gave no exterior hint of the revolution taking place in its lining. The operation went smoothly. The colon was first liberated from its attachments to the back of the abdomen. It yielded its position without resistance. Finally, I clamped the blood supply to the abdominal colon, killing it at last before it could kill Jon Tims. An hour and a half into the case, with the abdominal portion completed, I repaired to Jon's bottom. He was ignominiously propped up with his legs in the air, as if giving birth to his colon.

I cut around the hole and removed the anus. The anus is a remarkable organ, capable of feeling the difference between solid, liquid and gas and able to let the last out without discharging the first two! At 10:30, Jon went to the recovery room and I went to the changing room, dictated the operative report and headed for the office, stopping to reassure Mrs. Tims that all had gone well. It was the last time for the next thirty days that I could tell her that. I did not know what was in store for Jon or, for that matter, what the future held for Reggie Richards.

Reggie Richards was another matter. He was betrayed by a "friend." He and his 16-year-old classmates were just fooling around, showing off to the girls. The single bullet entered the abdomen just below his rib cage on the right.

In the rural hospital emergency room, a nurse, a Vietnam veteran, noted that the exit wound from his back was small, indicating "a small missile with relatively low muzzle velocity." Although this country hospital was not a trauma center, the patient was thought to be too unstable to survive the ambulance or even helicopter ride to the city. The surgeon on call opened the abdomen, scooped out the blood and found the injury.

He called three days later. "I need to transfer a boy, a gunshot wound," he said. He had found the bullet's path to be treacherous. It had entered the duodenum, severed the bile duct and exploded into the head of the pancreas. The area of damage was not large—just a few inches in diameter—but it was strategic. The stomach empties directly into the duodenum where the carefully choreographed business of digestion begins with the flow of bile from the liver and pancreatic juice from the pancreas. The bile duct and pancreatic ducts carry up to a quart of fluid a day into the duodenum where their respective openings are just a few tenths of an inch apart. A low-energy bullet had severed this beautifully coordinated but seldom thought-about biological nexus. It's where pasta salad becomes energy, muscle, life.

Although it's not often necessary, the surgeon felt the only way to stop the bleeding and to save Reggie's life was to remove the duodenum, part of the stomach, the head of the pancreas and the most distant part of the bile duct. The Whipple operation. He sutured the open bile duct into a piece of intestine, did the same with the pancreas, and finally, early in the morning, connected the stomach to the intestine.

Even before that long and complex operation was over, there were troubles. The bleeding continued. In fact, it never really slowed down. But since there was nothing more to do, the surgeon closed Reggie up.

Eight hours later, he re-explored the abdomen for bleeding and 24 hours after that he operated on Reggie again because "he wasn't doing well." The next day the frequently used wound fell apart and bile began to drain and the doctor made his call to me.

Reggie arrived on a Friday afternoon. (This is a common time for transfers to university teaching services. The university has round-the-clock resident surgeon coverage and that is not available to the private practice surgeon facing a long weekend with a very sick boy in a small hospital.) Reggie would not look at me or speak to me. Tired and fearing for his life, he couldn't say so or show it. We took off the dressings. The wound had split apart. It was twelve inches long and six wide. No organ was identifiable in its depth. Bile seeped up, green and yellow and ominous. There were some hills, some valleys, some pulsations, some pus, but nothing you could call liver or pancreas or stomach. It looked like a moist terrarium. This was not a science fiction film. It looked menacing. He was assigned a hospital room next to Jonathan Tims.

Jon was about ten days post-op when Reggie was admitted. He should have begun passing stool into the bag several days ago, but he hadn't. X-rays of his abdomen showed some dilated loops of bowel; we couldn't tell if the intestine, which is usually paralyzed for three to four days after an operation, had become obstructed or if the paralysis was just lasting longer than usual. Jon was impatient. He wanted that damn tube out of his nose. Over the next few days it became apparent that Jonathan Tims's small bowel was obstructed. His referring gastroenterologist kept calling me, asking me what was wrong. I was reluctant to admit it, but the evidence accumulated. I wanted to believe that the job I had done could not go wrong. But it had. A short section of small intestine had become twisted and blocked. His second operation was more difficult than the first. I found lots of inflammation and adhesions, caused by me a fortnight ago. In time the bowel was freed up and we closed. I dreaded phoning the gastroenterologist who had been right about the need for a second operation. I'd have to tell him he was right, that I had denied the evidence. I felt small.

Still, despite my admitted humiliation, Jonathan did not do well. He developed a fever. He was weak. His intestines opened up but he had no appetite. He hurt.

To find the source of his fever, multiple bacterial cultures were done of his blood, and his sputum and his urine and his stool. His blood cultures were positive, his heart murmur returned; the heart valves were infected again. This time Tims knew how long six weeks of antibiotics was. He became profoundly depressed.

As I saw him each day, I felt impotent and troubled: What will happen to this poor man next?

Actually, catastrophe struck first next door. I was out playing softball with the hospital team. We had a great time. I was the oldest but I was tolerated at first base where I couldn't get into much trouble. We had very snappy uniforms. About 8:30, I got a page and then the beeper went off again right away. Three times in a row—a sure sign something big was up.

Reggie Richards was bleeding. He vomited a bucketful of blood and then went into shock. Now blood was pouring out of his abdomen. I rushed to the hospital, uniform, cleats and all.

When I arrived, there was pandemonium. Nurses were stuffing towels into Reggie's open abdomen, hoping that pressure would slow the bleeding. But the towels saturated quickly and a pile of them, soaked dark greenish-red, was growing in the corner. The residents had inserted a breathing tube and large intravenous lines to deliver blood. Reggie was rapidly transfused. By the time I got there, he'd already had ten units of blood.

These nurses and residents were veterans of big-city, busy-hospital medicine. Not often were they surprised, much less frightened. But I sensed right away that things were out of control and nobody knew what to do.

I didn't either. When I took the towels out of Reggie's belly, blood filled up the abdomen as fast as water in a toilet bowl. I couldn't see the bleeding site. The abdominal contents were mush. The same enzymes that digest steak after a big meal had been let loose in Reggie's abdomen; they had digested away the wall of a blood vessel and now Reggie was bleeding to death. There were only two questions: Which artery was bleeding and how do we stop it? I knew that to take Reggie to the operating room and attempt to sew the artery shut would be a futile exercise; the digested tissue in his abdomen would not hold suture. It would be like trying to sew wet tissue paper.

I could think of only one plan. If it did not work, I had no backup strategy. We took Reggie to the radiology suite where a catheter was threaded through the femoral artery up into the abdominal aorta. Dye was injected and, on the fluoroscope screen, we would see it collect in the mid-abdomen. It looked like the blood was coming from the artery that had been tied off at his original operation—the gastroduodenal artery which brings blood, as its names suggests, to the stomach and duodenum. Now, if we could just manipulate the catheter out into the gastroduodenal artery, we could inject some coils to occlude the artery— and maybe stop the bleeding. By now Reggie had had 25 units of blood.

The catheter would not go out into the gastroduodenal artery. Reggie was thrashing about, making the job harder. He was still in shock. Finally, the catheter flipped into position. We injected. We stood back. The bleeding slowed. His blood pressure came up.

The plan, the only plan, had worked.

My uniform and cleats were soaked with blood.

The next day as we watched the 16-year-old slowly inch back from the brink, I said to a resident: "You know, if he'd been older he wouldn't have survived."

"Hey," he said, "if he'd been 17, he wouldn't have survived."

Jonathan Tims endured his six weeks. He was depressed but by the third week he had begun to read the newspaper again. He ate a little. His intestine worked. His temperature came down. Toward the end of the fifth week his neck started to swell, then his arm, then his face. Now what?

The superior vena cava, the vein that carries all the blood back to the heart from the head and neck and arms, was clotted off. If the swelling continued, his airway might obstruct, in which case he would need a hole cut into the trachea and a tube passed into it through the neck: a tracheostomy.

My God, what next? That's what I felt. That's what Jon felt. That's what his wife felt. But they helped. Tempered by his awful fortune, Jonathan had learned not to kick and scream. This complication, dire as it was, seemed easier. We started to anticoagulate (thin out) his blood so that the clot might shrink. Within a few days the swelling went down. Jon went home nine weeks after he had been admitted for a 7–10-day stay.

He got better.

So, too, did Reggie Richards. In time his wound began to close. The leakage of bile and pancreatic juice slowed own. He was depressed. He was fed by vein. His weight improved. Three months after the night he almost bled to death, he went home, still on intravenous feedings.

I knew that, ultimately, I'd have to operate on Reggie. I would get x-ray studies first, so I'd know where the end of the stomach and the bile duct and pancreas were. Then, after the inflammation died down, I could go in there and try to hook everything back together. It would not be easy.

Six months later we did get those x-rays. And we saw a remarkable thing: The stomach had somehow connected itself to the small bowel! The bile duct drained into the intestine! He had healed together. As improbably as winning the lottery, his body had healed and regenerated in just the right way, getting the equivalent of all six numbers just right. I suggested we try to feed Reggie by mouth. He had a cheeseburger.

Reggie gained back his weight and went back to school the next year. He had missed a year of his life. Next spring I got an invitation to his high school graduation.

Reggie and Jonathan each come to see me once a year now, as much for my benefit as for theirs.

One year they happened to come on the same day. As I watched from down the hall, I saw them approach each other—one man with the worst possible survivable luck and one boy with the most luck I had ever seen—and I wondered: If they touched, would there be a small explosion and they'd both be gone?